THIS BOOK IS YOURS TO KEEP
COMPLIMENTS OF NCC
OR PASS IT ON WHEN YOU ARE DONE

SO-AIL-730

Great Figures in History

Nelson Mandela

Rolihlahla (Nelson) Mandela

Y. kids
www.myykids.c

NCCJ

Advancing Equality.
Promoting Justice.
Building Community.

820A Prospect Hill Rd.
Windsor, CT 06095
www.nccj.org

Great Figures in History

Nelson Mandela

Copyright © 2008 YoungJin Singapore Pte. Ltd.
World rights reserved. No part of this publication may be stored in a retrieval system, transmitted, or reproduced in any way, including but not limited to photocopies, photographs, magnetic data, or other records, without the prior agreement and written permission of the publisher.

ISBN: 978-981-057551-9
Printed and bound in the Republic of Korea.

How to contact us
E-mail: feedback@myykids.com

Credits
Adaptation & Art: SAM (Special Academic Manga)
Production Manager: Suzie Lee
Editorial Services: Publication Services, Inc.
Developmental Editor: Rachel Lake, Publication Services, Inc.
Editorial Manager: Lorie Donovan, Publication Services, Inc.
Book Designer: SAM (Special Academic Manga)
Cover Designer: Litmus
Production Control: Misook Kim, Sangjun Nam

With the participation of

mda
Media Development Authority
Singapore

A Message to Readers

Welcome to the **Great Figures in History** series by Y. kids. These biographies of some of the world's most influential people will take you on an exciting journey through history. These are the stories of great scientists, leaders, artists, and inventors who have shaped the world we live in today.

How did these people make a difference in their world? You will see from their stories that things did not always come easily for them. Just like many of us, they often had problems in school or at home. Some of them had to overcome poverty and hardship. Still others faced discrimination because of their religion, their gender, or the color of their skin. But all of these **Great Figures in History** worked tirelessly and succeeded despite many challenges.

Sing, an adventurer from Planet Mud, will be your guide through the lives of these famous historical figures. The people of Sing's planet are in great danger, facing a strange disease that drains their mental powers. To save the people of Planet Mud, Sing must travel through space and time and try to capture the mental powers of several **Great Figures in History**. Will Sing be successful in his journey? You will have to read to find out!

If you enjoy this story, visit our website, **www.myykids.com**, to see other books in the **Great Figures in History** series. You can also visit the website to let us know what you liked or didn't like about the book, or to leave suggestions for other stories you would like to see.

A Note To Parents and Teachers

Y. kids welcomes you to Educational Manga Comics. We certainly hope that your child or student will enjoy reading our books. The Educational Manga Comics present material in "manga" form, a comic story style developed in Japan that is enjoying enormous popularity with young people today. These books deliver substantive educational content in a fun and easy-to-follow visual format.

At the end of each book, you will find bonus features—including a historical timeline, a summary of the individual's enduring cultural significance, and a list of suggested Web and print resources for related information—to enhance your reader's learning experience. Our website, **www.myykids.com**, offers supplementives activitional, resources, and study material to help you incorporate Y. kids books into your child's reading at home or in the classroom curriculum.

Our entire selection of Educational Manga Comics, covering math, science, history, biographies, and literature, is available on our website. The website also has a feedback option, and we welcome your input.

CONTENTS

WHO'S WHO?

Young Mandela

NELSON MANDELA

The first black president of South Africa, he has won the Nobel Peace Prize and was a great political leader. Courage, determination, mercy, and reconciliation were his political convictions.

GADLA HENRY MPHAKANYISWA

He was Nelson Mandela's father. He was also the chief of the town of Mvezo and council of the Thembu dynasty. He was tall, had a good build, and was dark-skinned. He was also wise and had oratorical talent but was stubborn.

NOSEKENI FANNY

Third wife of Gadla, she was a devoted Methodist.

WINNIE

Originally named Nomzamo Winifred Madikizela, she was a South African social worker and activist who was very politically active after her marriage to Mandela.

WALTER SISULU

Six years older than Mandela, lawyer Walter Sisulu was a friend and colleague who stood by Mandela's side during the struggle against apartheid.

OLIVER TAMBO

One of Nelson Mandela's closest friends, he was the head of the African National Congress and worked with Nelson Mandela for racial freedom in South Africa.

EVELYN NTOKO MASE

She was Mandela's first wife. She was a woman of little words and was attractive. She was a nurse and had four children with Mandela, but they got divorced due to the multiple strains of his absence.

The residents of Planet Mud in the Andromeda Galaxy have been suffering from a strange illness.

The Planet Mud Disease Control Committee has reported that this plague was caused by a so-called Confusion Virus that drains mental energy from people. Once affected by the virus, people suffer strange symptoms such as tiredness and frustration.

The Planet Mud Disease Control Committee has suggested a solution to this plague. They hope to clone aspects of the mental energy from some of the greatest souls of Planet Earth. When the Cam-cam records the lives of the great souls, it can collect copies of their unique and special mental energy. This mental energy is then refined into crystallized mental energy to be injected into the suffering residents of Planet Mud.

It is Sing's job to distill the crystallized fairy of each great soul's mental energy.

Sing An explorer from Planet Mud. He was dispatched by the Planet Mud Disease Control Committee to collect mental energies from the great souls of Planet Earth.

Alpha Plus Sing's assistant robot, who keeps him out of trouble. His vast store of information can solve many questions during their adventures.

Cam-cam An invention from Planet Mud. When it records the lives of the great people, their mental energy is copied and refined.

Determination Fairy When dusted with the powder from this fairy, people gain the will and courage to overcome obstacles and finish what they have started.

7

PROLOGUE

WE'RE GOING TO BE LATE! HURRY, HURRY!

I KNEW IT. I'VE BEEN TRYING TO WAKE YOU UP!

LET'S GO!

Union building, Pretoria, South Africa

On May 10, 1994, at its administrative capital, South Africa held one of the most important ceremonies in its history.

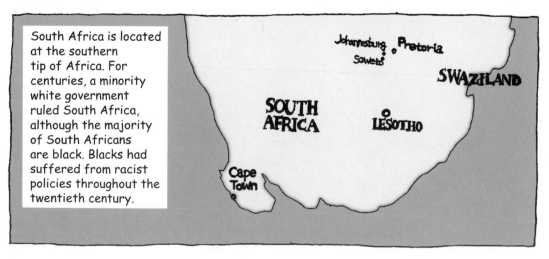

South Africa is located at the southern tip of Africa. For centuries, a minority white government ruled South Africa, although the majority of South Africans are black. Blacks had suffered from racist policies throughout the twentieth century.

Johannesburg Pretoria
Soweto

SWAZILAND

SOUTH AFRICA

LESOTHO

Cape Town

This ceremony was being held to celebrate the nation's first democratic elections in which citizens of all skin colors were allowed to vote.

World leaders, the press, and many others attended.

They were waiting for the hero of the day to announce the future of South Africa.

UGH!

SCREECH!

WE'RE NOT LATE FOR THE CEREMONY, ARE WE?

BY THE WAY, WHERE IS THE PERSON WE ARE LOOKING FOR? I CAN'T SEE ANYONE PARTICULARLY...

THAT MAN, OVER THERE.

THAT MAN?

HE LOOKS LIKE AN ORDINARY OLD MAN. WHAT IS ALL THIS FUSS ABOUT?

LADIES AND GENTLEMEN, THANK YOU FOR COMING.

THIS IS WHY YOU SHOULD HAVE READ THE DATA BEFORE WE LEFT!

WELL, I'M READING NOW. STOP NAGGING ME!

WELL, JUST BE SURE YOU DON'T MISS HIS SPEECH.

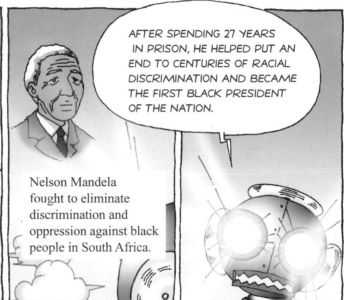

AFTER SPENDING 27 YEARS IN PRISON, HE HELPED PUT AN END TO CENTURIES OF RACIAL DISCRIMINATION AND BECAME THE FIRST BLACK PRESIDENT OF THE NATION.

Nelson Mandela fought to eliminate discrimination and oppression against black people in South Africa.

NOW, HE IS ABOUT TO GIVE HIS INAUGURATION SPEECH WHILE THE WORLD IS WATCHING.

HE BECAME PRESIDENT AFTER 27 YEARS IN PRISON? WOW, HE MUST BE A BRAVE MAN.

THERE ARE MANY MORE GREAT THINGS ABOUT HIM.

NELSON MANDELA TRULY LOVES PEACE. HE FORGAVE AND COMPROMISED WITH THE WHITE PEOPLE WHO HAD SUPPRESSED HIS CULTURE FOR HUNDREDS OF YEARS.

NOW IS NOT THE TIME FOR US TO FIGHT AND DISPUTE. WE SHOULD RECOVER FROM THE WOUNDS WE ARE CARRYING AND BECOME ONE.

WE WILL BUILD A SOCIETY IN WHICH ALL SOUTH AFRICANS, BOTH BLACK AND WHITE, CAN LIVE IN HARMONY—A RAINBOW NATION AT PEACE WITH ITSELF AND THE WORLD.

HURRAY!

HURRAY FOR SOUTH AFRICA!

LONG LIVE MANDELA!

HURRAY!

HURRAY!

HURRAY FOR SOUTH AFRICA!

HURRAY! LET'S CELEBRATE WITH MANDELA!

HURRAY, MANDELA!

CALM DOWN! WE ARE ON A MISSION TO COLLECT HIS SPIRITUAL ENERGY.

OH, I ALMOST FORGOT.

I HAVE TO WORK HARD TO KEEP MY MASTER ON TASK.

WELL, BEFORE WE COLLECT HIS SPIRITUAL ENERGY, I WOULD LIKE TO LEARN MORE ABOUT NELSON MANDELA.

LET'S GO TO SOUTH AFRICA, 1918.

HONG ON!

13

EPISODE 1
YOUNG ROLIHLAHLA

Village of Mvezo in the Transkei region, cape of South Africa.

IS THIS THE HOMETOWN OF NELSON MANDELA?

YES, THIS IS A PEACEFUL, RURAL VILLAGE

WHERE IS HIS HOUSE?

WAAAA WAAA

OH, THANK YOU!

THAT MUST BE THE PLACE! LET'S GO!

CONGRATULATIONS, CHIEF HENRY! IT'S A BOY.

Gadla Henry Mphakanyiswa, Mandela's father

Mandela's family lived in a fertile valley near the Indian Ocean.

Mandela's father was a member of the royal Thembu family, a Xhosa-speaking tribe.

WHAT A PERFECT CHILD.

I WILL NAME YOU ROLIHLAHLA.

Nosekeni Fanny, Mandela's mother

Mandela's father had four wives. Mandela and his three younger sisters were born to Chief Henry's third wife.

WHY WOULD YOU WANT TO NAME THE BOY ROLIHLAHLA?

ROLIHLAHLA MEANS "TO PULL ON A TREE BRANCH." WHY DOES HIS MOTHER DISLIKE THE NAME?

BECAUSE IT ALSO MEANS "TROUBLEMAKER!"

Mandela's father was appointed chief of the village. He was also the respected adviser who helped elect the Thembu king and gave advice to the king.

THE OX YOU HAVE LOST IS IMPORTANT PROPERTY OF THE VILLAGE!

YOU MUST PAY FOR THE LOSS OR BE PUNISHED AND IMPRISONED.

CHIEF, PLEASE FORGIVE ME. I WILL NEVER MAKE THIS MISTAKE AGAIN.

THE LAW OF THIS VILLAGE SHOULD BE FAIR TO EVERYONE. YOU CANNOT BE AN EXCEPTION. YOU MUST PAY FOR THE OX OR TAKE THE PUNISHMENT. MAKE YOUR DECISION BY TOMORROW.

YOUR HONOR, I AM INNOCENT.

The servant was afraid of being punished. So he went to a white judge of the region and lied to him.

I WAS SET UP FOR LOSING THIS OX, AND I HAVE BEEN TREATED UNFAIRLY BY THE VILLAGE CHIEF.

I SEE. I WILL HANDLE IT.

CHIEF HENRY MUST COME TO COURT.

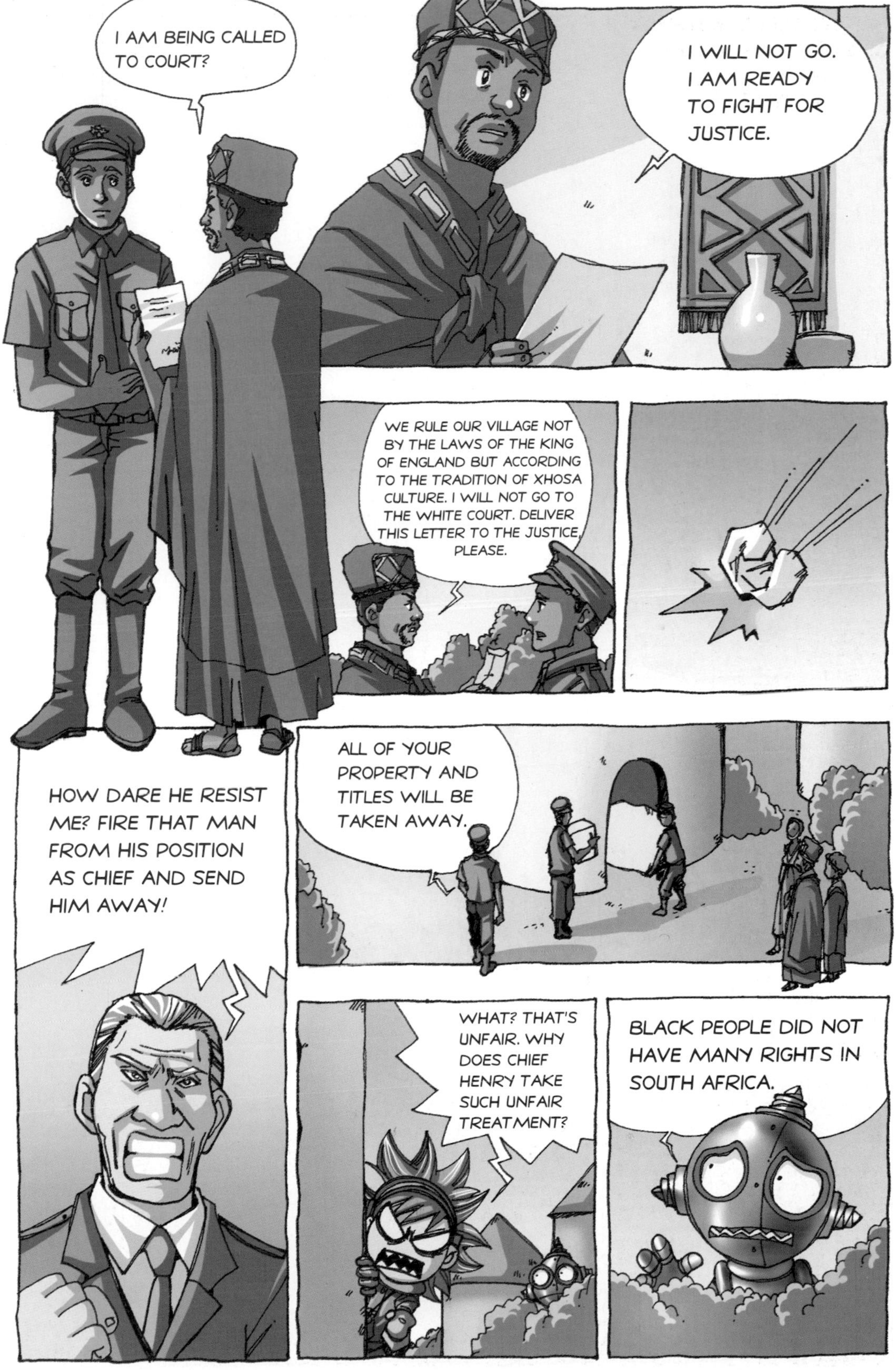
I AM BEING CALLED TO COURT?
I WILL NOT GO. I AM READY TO FIGHT FOR JUSTICE.
WE RULE OUR VILLAGE NOT BY THE LAWS OF THE KING OF ENGLAND BUT ACCORDING TO THE TRADITION OF XHOSA CULTURE. I WILL NOT GO TO THE WHITE COURT. DELIVER THIS LETTER TO THE JUSTICE, PLEASE.
HOW DARE HE RESIST ME? FIRE THAT MAN FROM HIS POSITION AS CHIEF AND SEND HIM AWAY!
ALL OF YOUR PROPERTY AND TITLES WILL BE TAKEN AWAY.
WHAT? THAT'S UNFAIR. WHY DOES CHIEF HENRY TAKE SUCH UNFAIR TREATMENT?
BLACK PEOPLE DID NOT HAVE MANY RIGHTS IN SOUTH AFRICA.

WHEN MANDELA WAS YOUNG, SOUTH AFRICA WAS RULED BY ENGLAND. THE GOVERNMENT OF ENGLAND HAD A JUSTICE OF THE PEACE IN EACH DISTRICT OF SOUTH AFRICA.

ALL TRIBAL MEMBERS, INCLUDING THE TRIBAL CHIEFS, HAD TO OBEY THE COLONIAL GOVERNMENT.

THE WHITE GOVERNMENT MAY TAKE AWAY MY PROPERTY AND POSITION AS A TRIBAL CHIEF. HOWEVER, IT CANNOT CHANGE MY MIND. I DID NOTHING WRONG. AS CHIEF OF MY TRIBE, I HAVE TO PROTECT OUR TRADITION AND CULTURE.

BUT HOW WILL WE SURVIVE? WE HAVE NOTHING. WE SHOULD MOVE NEAR MY PARENTS. THEIR VILLAGE WILL HELP US.

When Mandela was very young, his family moved to Qunu, a valley village north of Mvezo. It was surrounded by a clean stream and green plants.

Town of Qunu

At Qunu, Mandela's family made a living by farming and raising livestock.

GOOD-BYE, MOTHER.

TAKE CARE OF YOURSELF, SON.

HI! WHAT DO YOU WANT TO DO TODAY?

At the age of five, Mandela was responsible for taking care of cattle, sheep, and goats.

LET'S SWIM WHILE THE CATTLE ARE GRAZING. I WILL TEACH YOU HOW TO DO THE BUTTERFLY STROKE. WHEN WE FEEL HUNGRY, WE CAN CATCH SOME FISH.

Nelson Mandela remembers his early life in Qunu as the most precious time of his boyhood. He spent his days experiencing nature, learning about Xhosa culture, and playing with his friends.

19

Mandela's father spent one week a month with each of his four wives.

I'M HOME!

YOUR FATHER HAS COME. LET'S HAVE DINNER TOGETHER.

HELLO, FATHER!

MR. MBEKELA VISITED US TODAY. HE SAID THAT ROLIHLAHLA IS SO SMART THAT HE MUST ATTEND SCHOOL.

I DID NOT RECEIVE ANY FORMAL EDUCATION, AND NEITHER DID MY PARENTS. BUT IF MY CHILDREN WANT TO LEARN IN THE MISSIONARY SCHOOLS, I WILL NOT STOP THEM. LET'S ALLOW ROLIHLAHLA TO ATTEND SCHOOL.

SIGH . . .

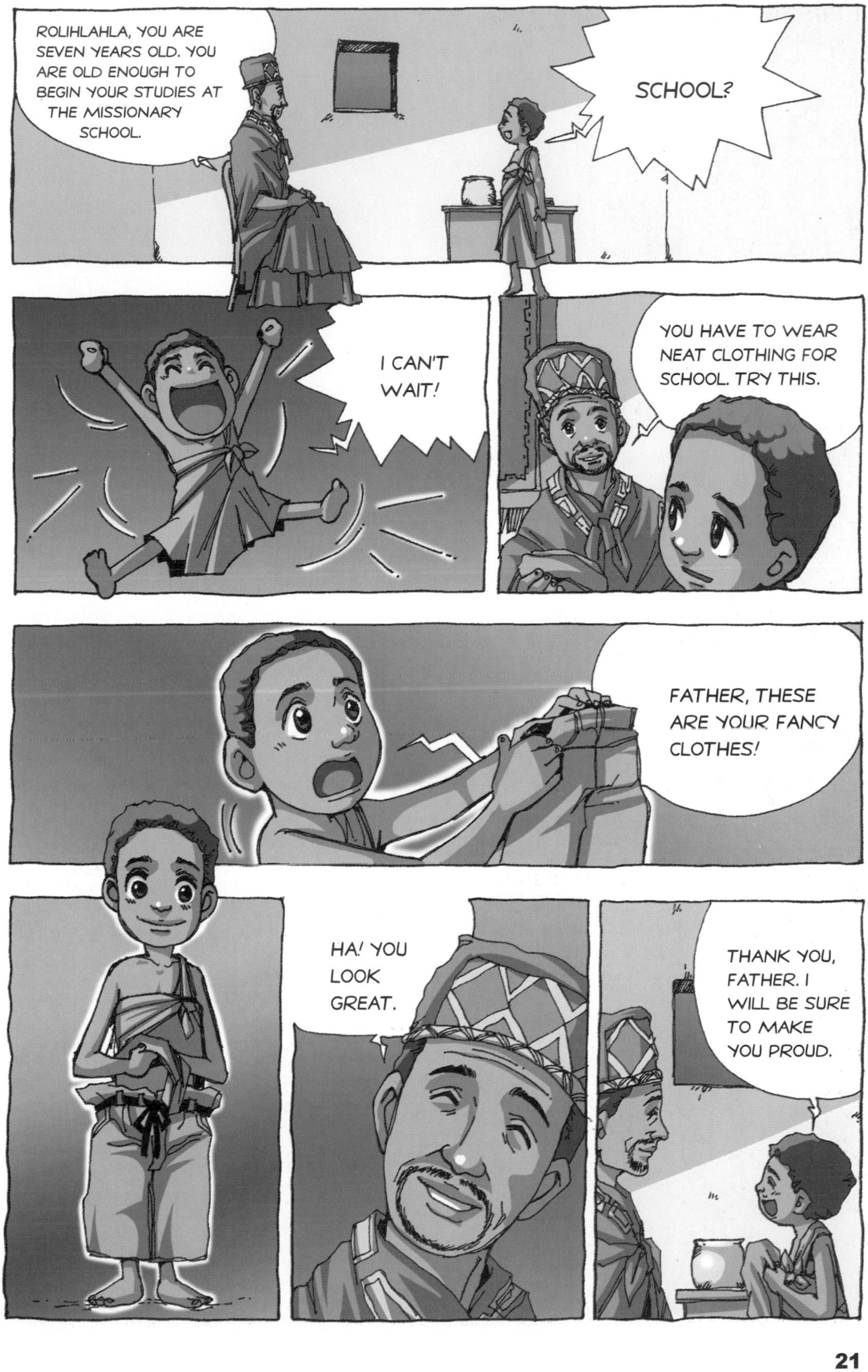
ROLIHLAHLA, YOU ARE SEVEN YEARS OLD. YOU ARE OLD ENOUGH TO BEGIN YOUR STUDIES AT THE MISSIONARY SCHOOL.
SCHOOL?
I CAN'T WAIT!
YOU HAVE TO WEAR NEAT CLOTHING FOR SCHOOL. TRY THIS.
FATHER, THESE ARE YOUR FANCY CLOTHES!
HA! YOU LOOK GREAT.
THANK YOU, FATHER. I WILL BE SURE TO MAKE YOU PROUD.

GOOD MORNING, TEACHER!

WELCOME TO OUR CLASS.

WHAT IS YOUR NAME?

MY NAME IS ROLIHLAHLA MANDELA.

ROLIH...

DO YOU HAVE AN ENGLISH NAME?

NO, I DON'T.

WELL, THEN, I WILL CALL YOU NELSON. NELSON MANDELA.

At that time, white people didn't even bother to pronounce African names, thinking that they were uncivilized. They ignored African culture and thought that white culture was superior.

YOU HAVE TO USE YOUR ENGLISH NAME IN SCHOOL. UNDERSTOOD?

YES, MA'AM.

1927

When Mandela was nine years old, his family suffered a great loss.

ROLIHLAHLA, WHAT'S WRONG? YOU LOOK VERY UPSET.

MY FATHER IS VERY ILL. MY MOTHERS ARE NURSING HIM. BUT HE CAN'T EAT ANYTHING OR GET UP FROM HIS BED.

COME BACK HOME—PLEASE!

ARE YOU ALL RIGHT, FATHER?

I WANT TO SMOKE.

COUGH COUGH

NO, YOU SHOULDN'T! YOU ARE TOO SICK TO SMOKE.

MY CHEST FEELS HEAVY. I THINK I WILL FEEL BETTER IF I SMOKE.

WHAT CAN WE DO?

OKAY. TAKE A PIPE TO YOUR FATHER.

23

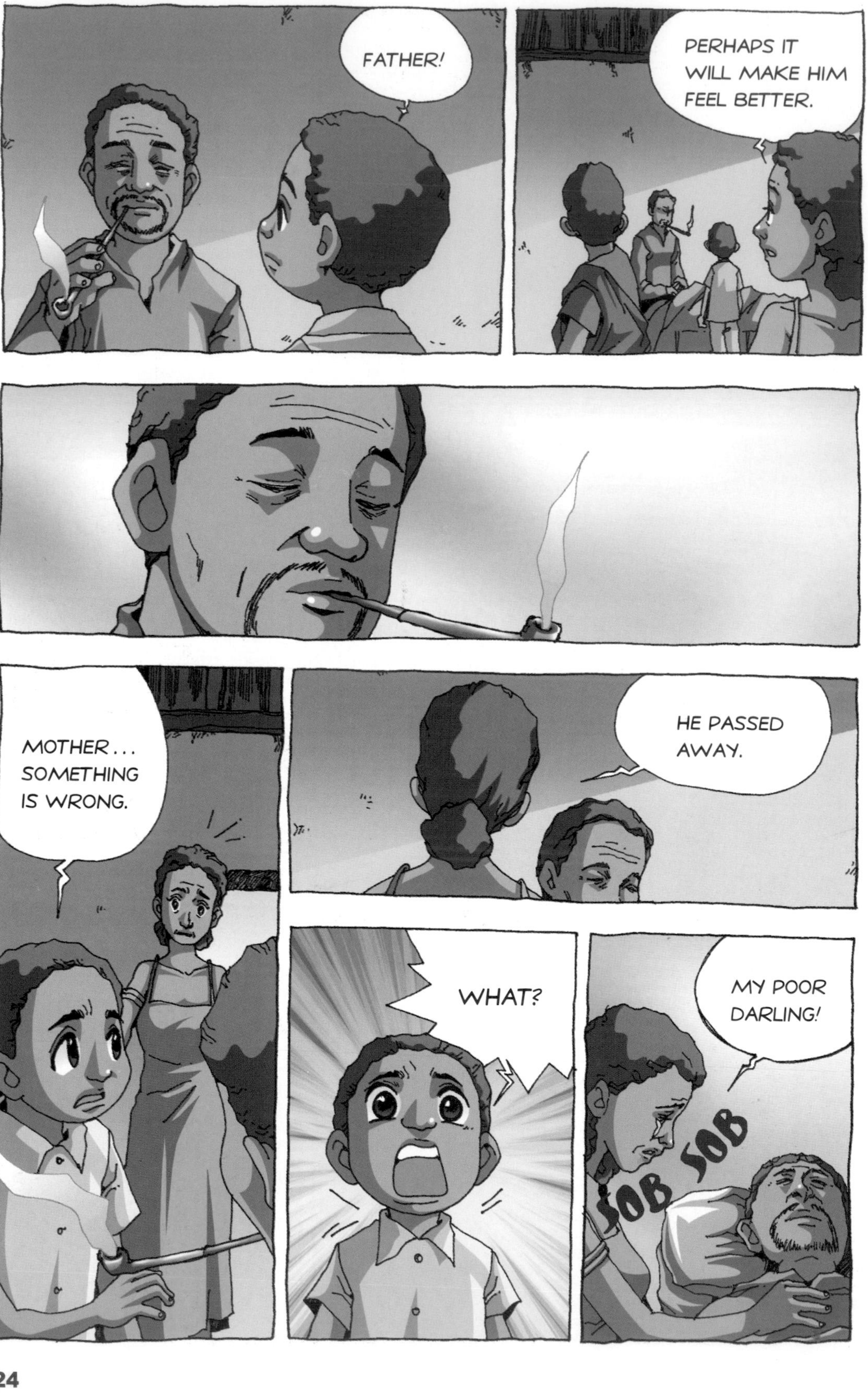
FATHER!
PERHAPS IT WILL MAKE HIM FEEL BETTER.
MOTHER... SOMETHING IS WRONG.
HE PASSED AWAY.
WHAT?
MY POOR DARLING!
SOB SOB

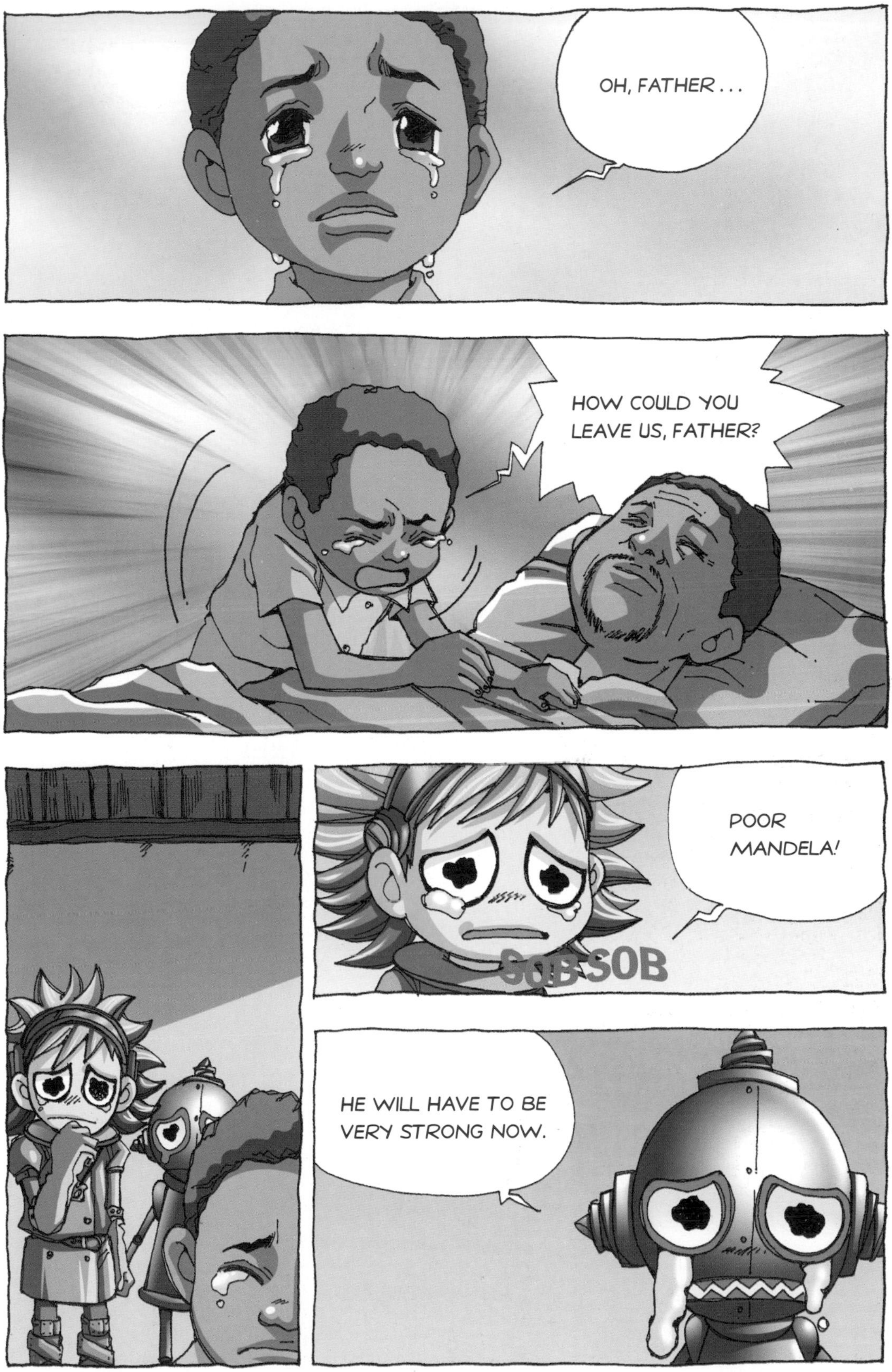
OH, FATHER . . .
HOW COULD YOU LEAVE US, FATHER?
POOR MANDELA!
SOB SOB
HE WILL HAVE TO BE VERY STRONG NOW.

EPISODE 2
CHIEF JONGINTABA'S PALACE

A few days after Mandela's father's funeral.

SON, YOU'D BETTER LEAVE THIS VILLAGE. CHIEF JONGINTABA OF THE THEMBU PEOPLE WILL TAKE CARE OF YOU NOW.

SIGH...

GOOD-BYE, QUNU! I WILL NEVER FORGET THIS PLACE.

The palace of Jongintaba Dalindyebo, the regent of the Thembu people.

HERE IS YOUR NEW HOME, THE CAPITAL OF THEMBULAND. CHIEF JONGINTABA AND HIS WIFE WILL RAISE YOU HERE.

OH, MY...

RING

Jongintaba was widely respected, and the colonial government left him much authority over his people.

HAIL, JONGINTABA! HAIL!

Chief Jongintaba Dalindyebo

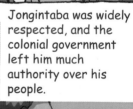

YOU MUST BE HENRY'S SON. WELCOME!

YES, SIR. I AM NELSON ROLIHLAHLA MANDELA.

YOUR FATHER WAS MY TRUSTED ADVISOR.

AND I WILL REPAY HIM BY TAKING YOU IN AS MY OWN CHILD.

NOW, I MUST RETURN TO QUNU. STUDY HARD AND GROW INTO A GREAT MAN. THAT'S YOUR FATHER'S WISH, TOO.

Although he was sad to see his mother depart, Mandela's heart was filled with excitement about his new life.

WORK HARD, MY SON!

MOTHER...

HURRAY!

He enjoyed everyday life at the royal household. It was like a magic palace to Mandela, and he shared everything with Jongintaba's own son, Justice.

HOW IS YOUR BOARDING SCHOOL, JUSTICE?

IT'S FUN. STUDYING IS A BIT BORING, OF COURSE, BUT I LIKE TO PLAY GAMES WITH MY FRIENDS.

JUSTICE IS VERY LUCKY. HE IS TALL AND GOOD AT SPORTS. EVERYBODY LIKES HIM. SOMEDAY, HE WILL BECOME THE LEADER OF THEMBU AFTER HIS FATHER.

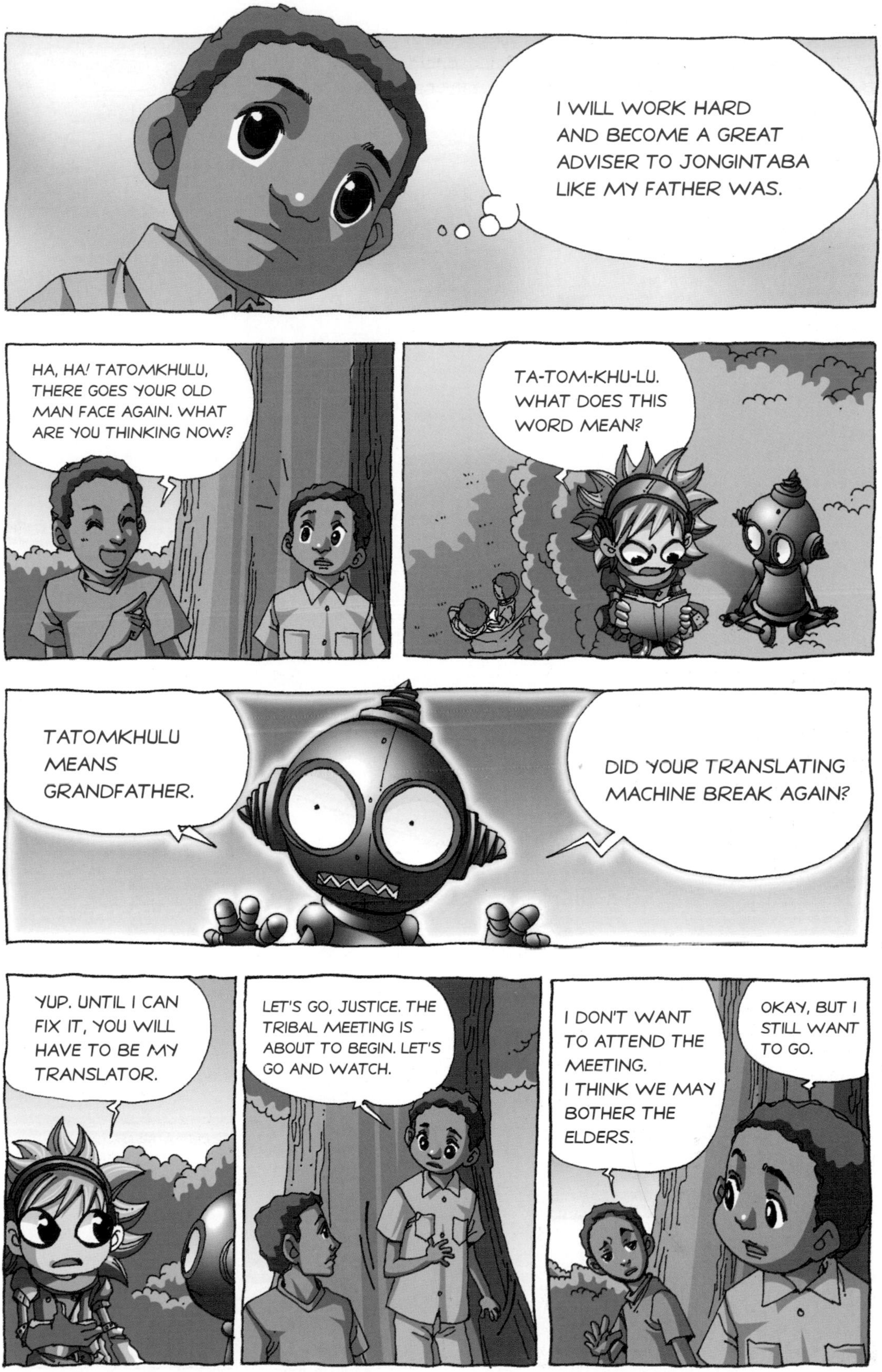
I WILL WORK HARD AND BECOME A GREAT ADVISER TO JONGINTABA LIKE MY FATHER WAS.
HA, HA! TATOMKHULU, THERE GOES YOUR OLD MAN FACE AGAIN. WHAT ARE YOU THINKING NOW?
TA-TOM-KHU-LU. WHAT DOES THIS WORD MEAN?
TATOMKHULU MEANS GRANDFATHER.
DID YOUR TRANSLATING MACHINE BREAK AGAIN?
YUP. UNTIL I CAN FIX IT, YOU WILL HAVE TO BE MY TRANSLATOR.
LET'S GO, JUSTICE. THE TRIBAL MEETING IS ABOUT TO BEGIN. LET'S GO AND WATCH.
I DON'T WANT TO ATTEND THE MEETING. I THINK WE MAY BOTHER THE ELDERS.
OKAY, BUT I STILL WANT TO GO.

Jongintaba's council held a tribal meeting whenever the Thembu people faced an important issue. All male residents in the community were allowed to attend the meeting.

Mandela loved to attend the tribal meetings. He ran errands for the elders and listened to what they had to say.

CHILD! RUN AND GET ME SOME WATER.

OKAY!

I WAS DISAPPOINTED BY JONGINTABA'S APPROACH AT THE LAST MEETING WITH THE GOVERNMENT. HE WAS NOT FORCEFUL ENOUGH.

I AGREE.

I THINK...

THE PEOPLE AT THE MEETINGS ARE SO OPEN ABOUT THEIR OPINIONS. THEY CRITICIZE OUR LEADER IF THEY THINK THAT HE DID SOMETHING WRONG, AND THE REGENT IS NOT ANGRY ABOUT IT.

HE LISTENS TO THE OPINIONS OF HIS PEOPLE WITH AN OPEN AND FAIR MIND. THE PEOPLE CAN BE HONEST WITH THEIR FEELINGS.

After people said their opinions freely, Jongintaba summed up the meeting and harmonized their opinions. He never forced any conclusions or opinions.

THIS IS THE END OF TODAY'S MEETING. A FESTIVAL BEGINS TODAY. EVERYONE, ENJOY THIS NIGHT OF SHARING, EATING, AND TALKING.

JONGINTABA, AREN'T YOU ANGRY ABOUT THOSE WHO CRITICIZED YOU?

MANDELA, A GREAT LEADER IS LIKE A SHEPHERD. AN EXCELLENT SHEPHERD NEVER LETS HIS SHEEP KNOW THAT THEY ARE BEING LED. THE PEOPLE LET ME BE THEIR LEADER BECAUSE THEY TRUST ME TO TAKE CARE OF THEM.

I HOPE THAT SOMEDAY I WILL BEHAVE AS WISELY AS JONGINTABA.

When the meeting was over, people spent their night talking about admirable heroes of Africa.

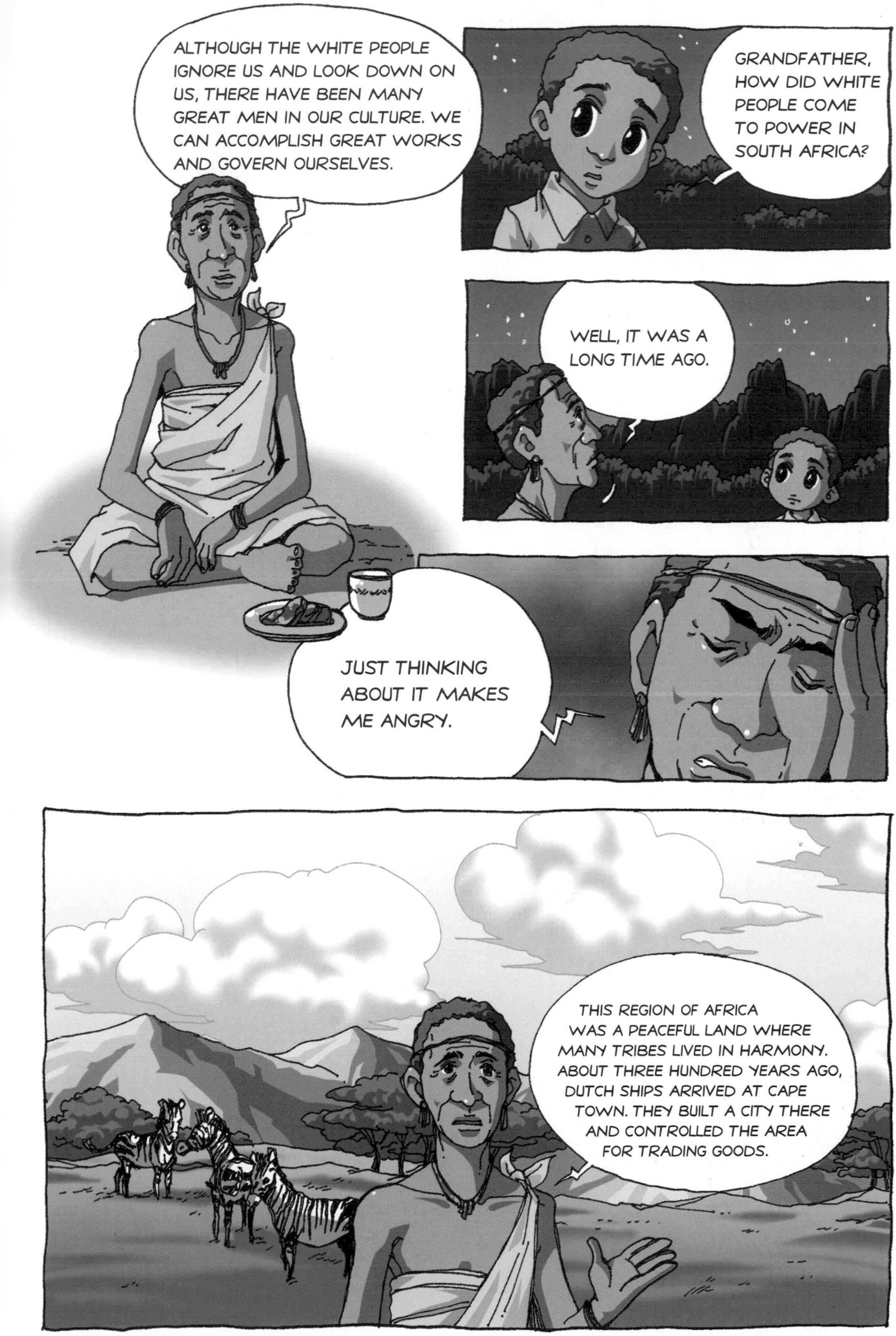
ALTHOUGH THE WHITE PEOPLE IGNORE US AND LOOK DOWN ON US, THERE HAVE BEEN MANY GREAT MEN IN OUR CULTURE. WE CAN ACCOMPLISH GREAT WORKS AND GOVERN OURSELVES.
GRANDFATHER, HOW DID WHITE PEOPLE COME TO POWER IN SOUTH AFRICA?
WELL, IT WAS A LONG TIME AGO.
JUST THINKING ABOUT IT MAKES ME ANGRY.
THIS REGION OF AFRICA WAS A PEACEFUL LAND WHERE MANY TRIBES LIVED IN HARMONY. ABOUT THREE HUNDRED YEARS AGO, DUTCH SHIPS ARRIVED AT CAPE TOWN. THEY BUILT A CITY THERE AND CONTROLLED THE AREA FOR TRADING GOODS.

THEY TOOK AWAY OUR LAND AND MADE IT THEIR FARMLAND, AND BROUGHT MANY PEOPLE FROM OTHER LANDS TO BE THEIR SLAVES! IN THE MEANTIME, DIAMOND AND GOLD MINES WERE FOUND IN AFRICA.

THEN, WHITE PEOPLE FROM OTHER NATIONS COMPETED TO OBTAIN OUR LAND. THE DESCENDENTS OF THE DUTCH SETTLERS ARE THE AFRIKANERS, AND THEY ARE THE LARGEST GROUP OF WHITES IN SOUTH AFRICA.

ENGLAND FINALLY GAINED CONTROL OF SOUTH AFRICA AND MADE IT A BRITISH COLONY.

WHITE PEOPLE BROUGHT MANY THINGS TO OUR CULTURE.

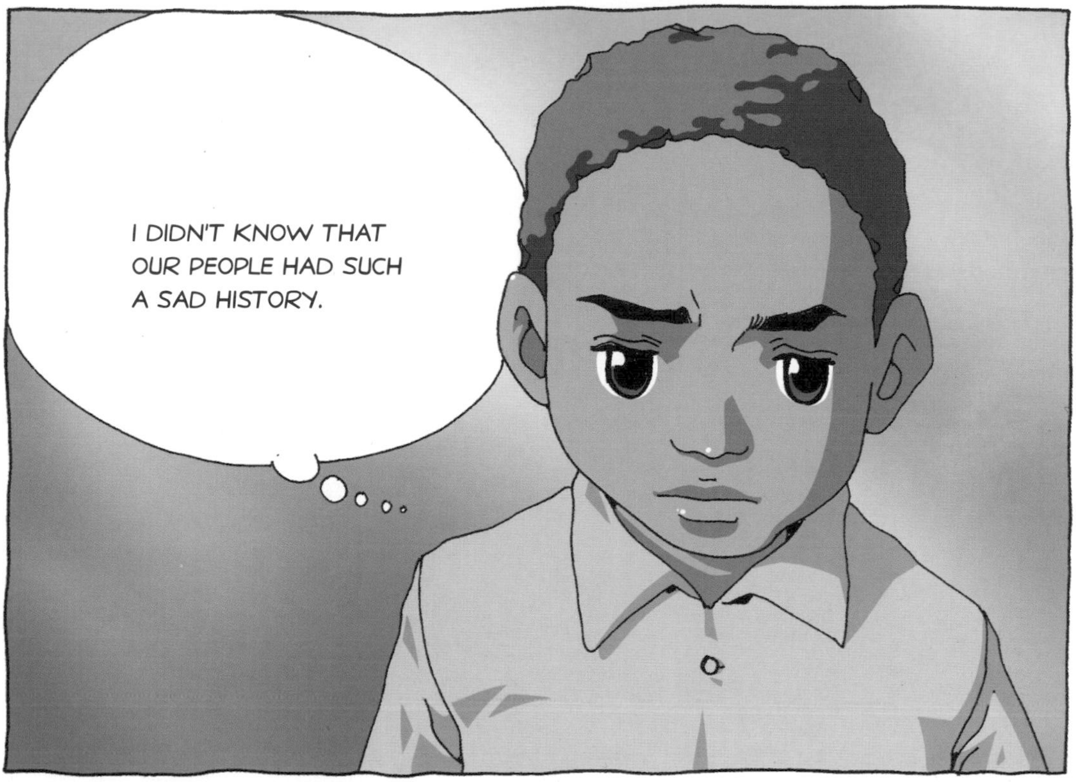
I DIDN'T KNOW THAT OUR PEOPLE HAD SUCH A SAD HISTORY.

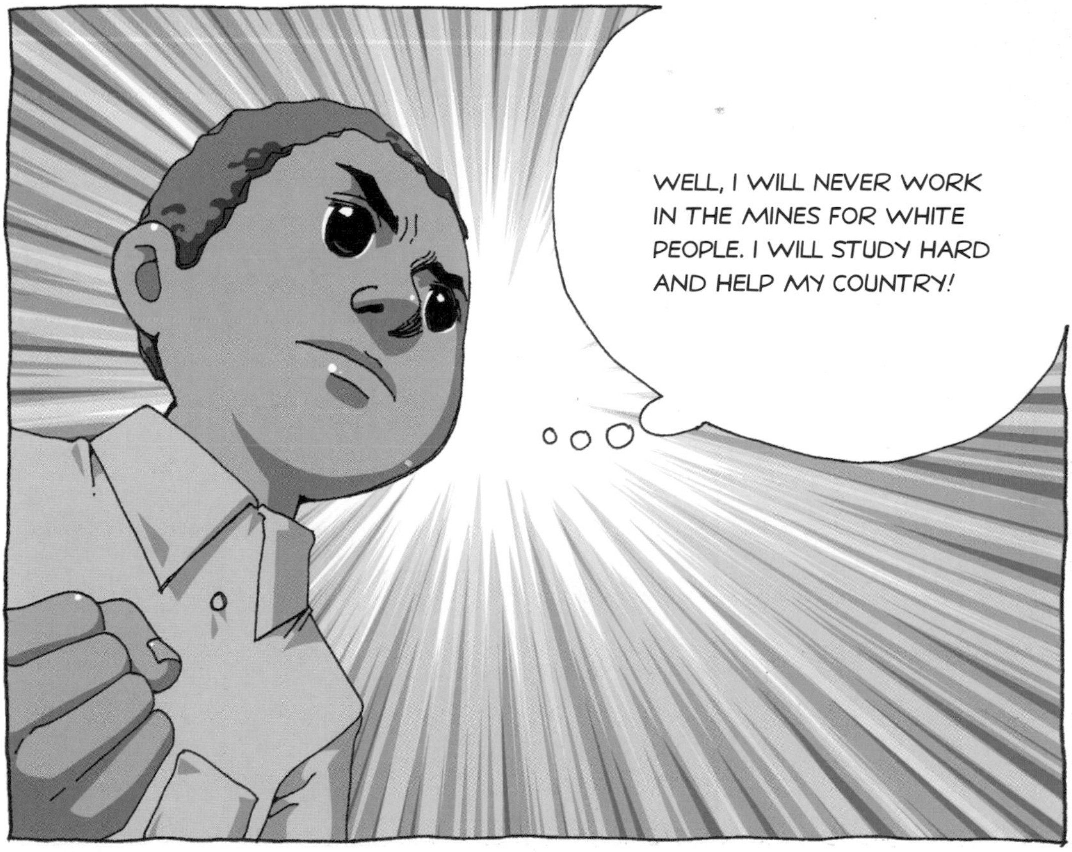
WELL, I WILL NEVER WORK IN THE MINES FOR WHITE PEOPLE. I WILL STUDY HARD AND HELP MY COUNTRY!

EPISODE 3
ROAD OF LEARNING

1934

When Nelson Mandela turned 16, he had a coming-of-age ceremony and entered Clarkebury Boarding Institute.

I AM PLEASED TO SEE YOU ATTEND A GOOD SCHOOL, MANDELA. I AM REALLY PROUD OF YOU.

THESE SHOES ARE A PRESENT FOR YOU.

THANK YOU, SIR!

MANDELA, I HAVE SOMETHING TO TELL YOU BEFORE YOU LEAVE YOUR HOME.

YOU SHOULD ALWAYS ACT WISELY AND BRAVELY, AND NEVER HUMILIATE OR HURT OTHERS. JUST STUDY HARD AND DO YOUR BEST.

THANK YOU, I WILL KEEP THAT IN MIND.

Clarkebury Boarding Institute

Founded in 1825, the Clarkebury school was the best mission school in Transkei. Mandela finished their three-year requirements in just two years.

Boarding school at Healdtown

Then he attended Healdtown, the biggest boarding school in sub-Saharan Africa.

1939, Fort Hare University

Fort Hare University was the best college for black people in South Africa. Fort Hare University was home to many great African scholars.

STARTING TODAY, I AM A STUDENT OF FORT HARE UNIVERSITY LAW SCHOOL.

MANDELA, YOU MADE IT! I AM HAPPY FOR YOU.

DO YOU LIKE THE SUIT? YOU LOOK GREAT IN THOSE CLOTHES.

THANK YOU SO MUCH. I DON'T DESERVE THIS.

I WILL WORK EVEN HARDER THAN BEFORE. I WILL BECOME A LAWYER TO WORK FOR JONGINTABA AND TO PLEASE MY MOTHER IN QUNU.

Nelson Mandela was busy studying law, English, anthropology, politics, and organizations for native Africans. At Fort Hare, he met his lifelong friend Oliver Tambo.

YOU ARE SO SMART, OLIVER. I HAVE A TOTALLY NEW PERSPECTIVE ABOUT EVERYTHING WHILE I AM LISTENING TO YOU.

Oliver Tambo

YOU OVERESTIMATE ME. YOU ARE MUCH WISER THAN I AM.

I AM STILL TRYING HARD TO GET ACCUSTOMED TO COLLEGE LIFE. I HAVE NEVER LIVED IN A CITY BEFORE, AND I HAVE NEVER WORN PAJAMAS OR USED A TOOTHBRUSH.

I REALLY AM A COUNTRY BOY. MY OLD LIFESTYLE MAY NOT HAVE HAD MANY LUXURIES, BUT I MISS THAT SIMPLE LIFE.

YOU REALLY ARE A COUNTRY FELLOW, BUT SO AM I. WE WILL BE GOOD FRIENDS!

Nelson Mandela studied hard to become one of South Africa's most promising students. But something unexpected happened during his second year.

At the end of his sophomore year, he was nominated for the Student Council at the university.

I HEARD THAT YOU ARE ONE OF THE NOMINEES, MANDELA.

YES. THE NOMINEES WILL HAVE A MEETING WITH THE STUDENTS THIS AFTERNOON. YOU'D BETTER COME.

STUDENTS, PLEASE SHARE YOUR THOUGHTS ABOUT FORT HARE WITH THE STUDENT COUNCIL.

THE CAFETERIA FOOD IS REALLY AWFUL. WE DEMAND BETTER FOOD.

THE STUDENT COUNCIL SHOULD BE STRONG ENOUGH TO FIX PROBLEMS THAT CONCERN STUDENTS.

IF THE UNIVERSITY DOES NOT GIVE THE STUDENT COUNCIL ANY REAL POWER, WE WILL NOT VOTE FOR THE STUDENT COUNCIL REPRESENTATIVES.

Many of the students did not participate in the voting. Only 25 students voted to elect 6 representatives.

Nelson Mandela was one of them.

ALTHOUGH WE WERE ELECTED, THE RESULTS OF THE ELECTION ARE INVALID BECAUSE MOST STUDENTS DID NOT PARTICIPATE IN VOTING.

SO WE MUST RESIGN.

However, Dr. Kerr, dean of Fort Hare, told the students to keep their positions or they would be expelled. The other five students remained on the Student Council.

NELSON, YOU WERE ELECTED AND IT WOULD BE IRRESPONSIBLE FOR YOU TO RESIGN. I WILL EXPEL YOU IF YOU RESIGN YOUR OFFICE. THINK ABOUT IT AND MAKE A DECISION BY TOMORROW.

WHAT AM I GOING TO DO? IF I GET EXPELLED, MY DREAM OF BECOMING A LAWYER WILL DISSOLVE, AND MY MOTHER AND JONGINTABA WILL BE SO DISAPPOINTED.

BUT I CANNOT LET DOWN THE STUDENTS WHO TRUSTED ME...

I WILL NOT LET DR. KERR CONTROL MY DESTINY. I MUST DO WHAT IS RIGHT AND RESIGN FROM THE POSITION.

I DON'T UNDERSTAND. IT SEEMS LIKE ACCEPTING THE POSITION IS THE EASIEST OPTION. WHAT IS HE WORRIED ABOUT?

WELL, YOU ARE A ROBOT AND YOU ALWAYS MAKE RATIONAL DECISIONS. BUT PEOPLE ARE NOT SO PREDICTABLE.

MANDELA COULD HAVE KEPT THE POSITION WITHOUT HURTING ANYONE, BUT HE STILL FELT THAT IT WAS WRONG.

PERHAPS HE WILL CHANGE HIS MIND.

ANYTHING IS POSSIBLE.

Eventually, Mandela was asked to leave Fort Hare University.

I BEHAVED ACCORDING TO MY MORALS. I AM PROUD OF MYSELF.

The royal Thembu household

MANDELA, IS IT TRUE THAT YOU WERE EXPELLED FROM THE UNIVERSITY?

YES, THAT'S RIGHT. HOWEVER, I DO NOT REGRET IT.

BUT IT WAS COMPLETELY FOOLISH. RETURN TO YOUR SCHOOL AND APOLOGIZE TO DEAN KERR. HE WILL ACCEPT YOU AGAIN.

NO. I WOULD BE ASHAMED OF MYSELF.

JUSTICE DROPPED OUT OF SCHOOL. AND NOW YOU GET EXPELLED? SHAME ON YOU!

I WILL HAVE TO TRY ANOTHER METHOD TO TEACH MY BOYS TO BE RESPONSIBLE MEN.

WHAT? MARRIAGE?

YES. HE ALSO WANTS ME TO MARRY A LOCAL GIRL. MY FATHER HAS ALREADY SENT COWS FOR MARRIAGE PAYMENT TO THE BRIDE'S FAMILY.

I CANNOT MARRY YET. MY DREAM IS FAR FROM ACCOMPLISHED, AND I DON'T WANT YOUR FATHER TO FIND ME A WIFE.

WE'D BETTER RUN AWAY FOR A WHILE TO WORK AND STUDY.

WHERE COULD WE GO?

TO JOHANNESBURG!

EPISODE 4
LAWYER IN JOHANNESBURG

Johannesburg, 1941

Johannesburg, the largest city in South Africa, was built in 1880s when gold was discovered there. By 1941, thousands of African people were seeking jobs in the big city.

WE WILL FIND SUCCESS IN THIS CITY, JUSTICE!

OF COURSE WE WILL!

YOU TWO ARE FIRED! GO BACK TO YOUR HOME!

PLEASE, WE NEED THE WORK.

PLEASE, WE NEED THE WORK.

Black person trade unionism

MY FATHER MUST BE VERY UPSET. DO WE HAVE TO GO BACK?

I AM NOT READY TO GO BACK. LET'S SPLIT UP FOR A WHILE. WE CAN GET A JOB EASIER IF WE SEPARATE.

Walter's office

Mandela met Walter Sisulu, a successful businessman who operated a real estate office in Johannesburg.

GOOD MORNING, MR. SISULU. I AM NELSON MANDELA.

NICE TO MEET YOU, MANDELA!

I THOUGHT THAT PEOPLE HAD TO GRADUATE FROM A UNIVERSITY TO ACHIEVE SUCCESS. BUT I WAS WRONG. MR. SISULU IS SO WISE AND CAPABLE, ALTHOUGH HE HAS NO UNIVERSITY DEGREE. WHAT A RESPECTABLE MAN HE IS!

SEARCH FOR WALTER SISULU AND TELL ME ABOUT HIM.

WALTER SISULU WAS BORN IN THE TRANSKEI REGION OF SOUTH AFRICA IN 1912. HE WAS A BLACK HUMAN RIGHTS ACTIVIST WHO FOUGHT AGAINST RACIAL DISCRIMINATION IN SOUTH AFRICA.

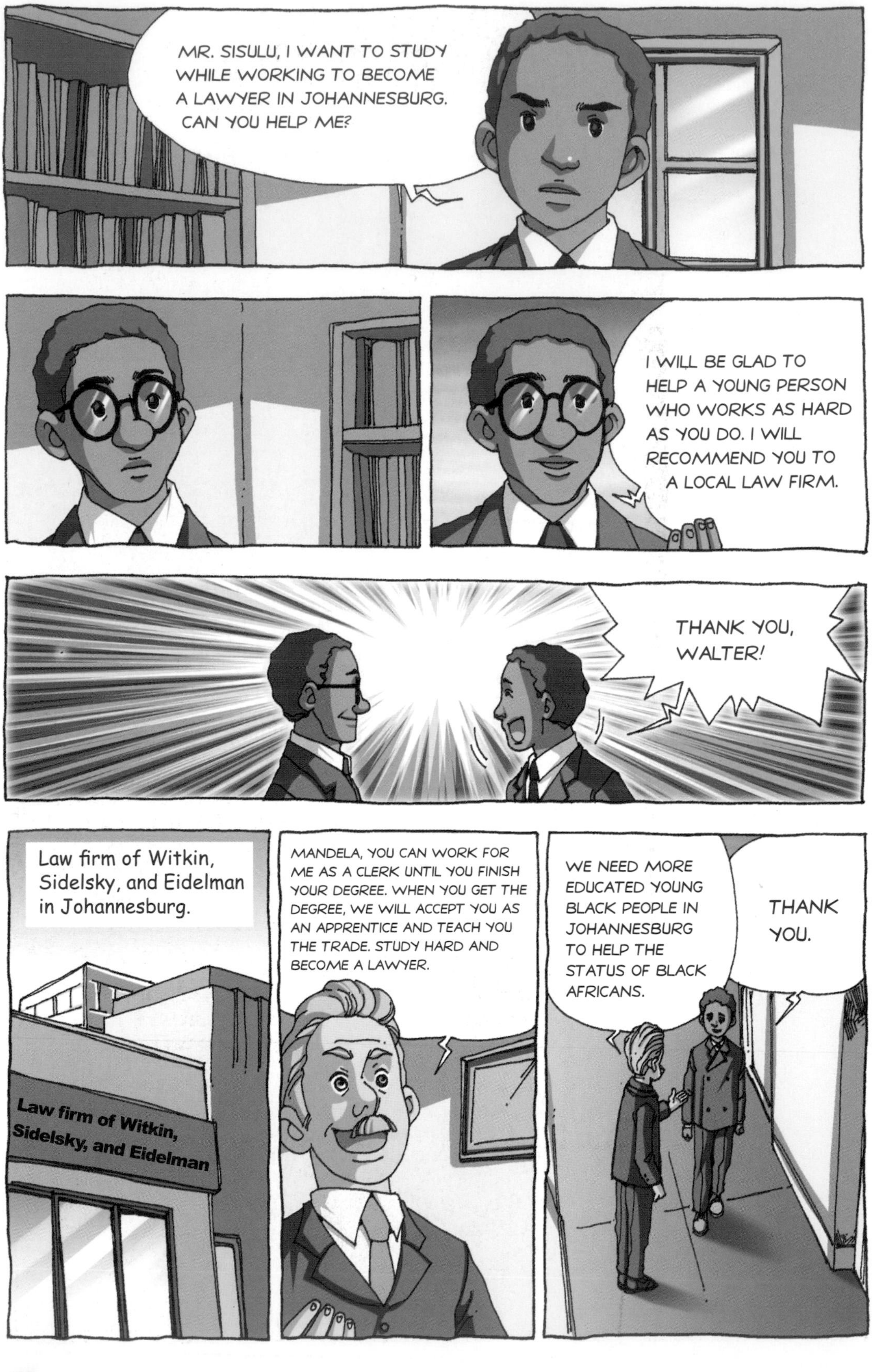
MR. SISULU, I WANT TO STUDY WHILE WORKING TO BECOME A LAWYER IN JOHANNESBURG. CAN YOU HELP ME?
I WILL BE GLAD TO HELP A YOUNG PERSON WHO WORKS AS HARD AS YOU DO. I WILL RECOMMEND YOU TO A LOCAL LAW FIRM.
THANK YOU, WALTER!
Law firm of Witkin, Sidelsky, and Eidelman in Johannesburg.
Law firm of Witkin, Sidelsky, and Eidelman
MANDELA, YOU CAN WORK FOR ME AS A CLERK UNTIL YOU FINISH YOUR DEGREE. WHEN YOU GET THE DEGREE, WE WILL ACCEPT YOU AS AN APPRENTICE AND TEACH YOU THE TRADE. STUDY HARD AND BECOME A LAWYER.
WE NEED MORE EDUCATED YOUNG BLACK PEOPLE IN JOHANNESBURG TO HELP THE STATUS OF BLACK AFRICANS.
THANK YOU.

MANDELA, THESE ARE YOUR COWORKERS.

HI. I AM MANDELA. IT'S MY PLEASURE TO WORK WITH YOU.

GAUR RADEBE WORKS FOR THE RIGHTS OF BLACK AFRICANS.

I WILL WORK HARD AND BE RECOGNIZED HERE. I WILL FINISH MY UNIVERSITY DEGREE AND BECOME A LAWYER.

Mandela was not allowed to live in Johannesburg because black people were forced to live in separate areas from the Dutch Afrikaners and people of British descent. Mandela rented a room in Alexandra, a run-down village far from the center of the city.

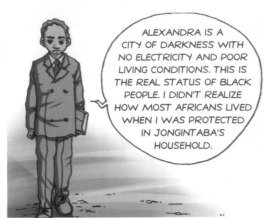

ALEXANDRA IS A CITY OF DARKNESS WITH NO ELECTRICITY AND POOR LIVING CONDITIONS. THIS IS THE REAL STATUS OF BLACK PEOPLE. I DIDN'T REALIZE HOW MOST AFRICANS LIVED WHEN I WAS PROTECTED IN JONGINTABA'S HOUSEHOLD.

BUT ALTHOUGH THIS PLACE HAS NO BATHROOMS OR CLEAN DRINKING WATER, AT LEAST THERE ARE NO WHITE PEOPLE TO OBEY.

I PAID THE RENT AND BOUGHT BOOKS AND CANDLES, BUT NOW I'VE RUN OUT OF MONEY AGAIN. TO SAVE MONEY, I CAN WALK TO WORK.

HEY! YOU!

YOU WANT TO FIGHT?

BANG

BOY, I CAN'T GO A DAY WITHOUT HEARING SOUNDS OF FIGHTING AND UNREST.

December 1942

CONGRATULATIONS, MANDELA! YOU FINALLY COMPLETED YOUR FIRST DEGREE.

THANK YOU, GAUR!

WE HOPE THAT AS MORE BLACK PEOPLE ARE EDUCATED, OUR SOCIAL STATUS WILL IMPROVE. BUT PERHAPS THAT IS NOT A REALISTIC SOLUTION.

YOU SEE? THERE IS A HUGE GAP BETWEEN THE LIVES OF WHITE PEOPLE AND BLACK PEOPLE. IT COULD TAKE A THOUSAND YEARS TO BRIDGE THE GAP IF WE ONLY OFFER BLACK PEOPLE MORE EDUCATION.

THEN WHAT IS THE REALISTIC SOLUTION?

THE AFRICAN NATIONAL CONGRESS CAN HELP SOLVE OUR PROBLEMS AND DRIVE CHANGE IN SOUTH AFRICA.

AFRICAN NATIONAL CONGRESS? I THINK I HEARD ABOUT IT AT FORT HARE UNIVERSITY.

WALTER SISULU, OUR BOSS, IS A MEMBER OF THE GROUP.

AND I, GAUR, AM ALSO A MEMBER.

HA, HA!

The branch of the African National Congress Society

District meeting of the African National Congress.

Mandela joined the African National Congress in 1943.

ALPHA PLUS, TELL ME MORE ABOUT THE AFRICAN NATIONAL CONGRESS. IT SOUNDS LIKE AN IMPORTANT ORGANIZATION.

I THINK YOU'RE SMARTER THAN YOU LOOK.

HEY!

THE AFRICAN NATIONAL CONGRESS...

...was the first organization to defend the rights of South Africa's black population. It was founded in 1912, and it is the oldest political group in the Republic of South Africa. It first used nonviolent resistance to protest the white minority rule.

WHY DO YOU WANT TO QUIT SO SUDDENLY?

THIS FIRM DOES NOT NEED BOTH OF US. YOU WILL BECOME A GREAT LAWYER.

I DO NOT HAVE MUCH INTEREST IN BEING A LAWYER. I WILL START A REAL ESTATE FIRM.

GAUR...

BUT...

HE SACRIFICES HIMSELF FOR ME AND THIS NATION.

After Gaur stopped working, Sidelsky promoted Mandela to be the company's apprentice.

Mandela finally started his law studies at the University of Witwatersrand.

In South Africa, black people suffered constant segregation (living separately) and discrimination.

WAA! WAA!

There were special hospitals for black people. They had to use specific buses and live within certain neighborhoods. They could only attend black schools and work for other black people in specific regions. Any time they wanted to travel out of the designated regions, they had to show a special pass. They could not live or travel freely, as white people could.

These experiences did not change Nelson Mandela into a human rights activist overnight. However, as he witnessed the suffering and misery of his people, he gradually became interested in helping to liberate the black Africans from oppression.

1944, Walter's house

MANDELA, THIS IS ANTON LEMBEDE, AND ASHBY MDA.

He was also inspired by the other young human rights activists he met in the African National Congress.

PLEASED TO MEET YOU!

NICE TO MEET YOU, MANDELA!

I HAVE HEARD A LOT ABOUT YOU FROM WALTER. YOU ARE STUDYING TO BECOME A LAWYER.

YES.

MANDELA, I AM NOT BLAMING YOU. I AM A LAWYER, TOO. BUT, HAVE YOU EVER THOUGHT THAT YOUNG AFRICANS ARE WORSHIPING AND FLATTERING WHITE PEOPLE, AND THAT THEY TRY TO BE ACCEPTED BY WHITE PEOPLE BECAUSE THEY THINK WESTERN CULTURE IS SUPERIOR?

OH ... I NEVER THOUGHT OF IT THAT WAY.

55

I THINK THAT WE CAN BE FREE ONLY WHEN WE RESPECT OURSELVES AND REVIVE OUR CULTURE. WHAT DO YOU THINK?

TO BE HONEST, I THOUGHT THAT THE STATUS OF BLACK PEOPLE WOULD IMPROVE WHEN MORE ELITE AFRICANS SUCCEED. BUT MAYBE THIS IS NOT TRUE.

I AM PROBABLY ONE OF THE ELITE AFRICANS WHO WANTS TO BE ACCEPTED BY WHITE PEOPLE, JUST AS LEMBEDE SAID.

African National Congress

Mandela gave up the dream of Africa's black elites closing the gap between blacks and whites. After that, he was active in the African National Congress meetings and protests.

Brilliant young men like Anton Lembede, Walter Sisulu, Oliver Tambo, and Nelson Mandela were members of the African National Congress. But they were frustrated by its strategy.

THE ANC HAS LOST TOUCH WITH THE LIVES OF ORDINARY AFRICAN PEOPLE.

They founded the ANC Youth League in 1944.

Walter's house became a haven for freedom activists and members of the African National Congress. It was always crowded with people having important discussions.

STOP DEBATING AND EAT SOMETHING, GENTLEMEN.

THANKS!

!

WHO IS THAT GIRL GIVING EVERYONE THE FOOD?

SHE IS WALTER'S COUSIN, EVELYN MASE. SHE IS TRAINING TO BECOME A NURSE. SHE'S VERY KIND.

MANDELA, ARE YOU ATTRACTED TO HER?

Evelyn and Mandela fell in love and married in 1944.

EVELYN, THIS IS A SHABBY HOUSE. I AM SORRY.

WHEREVER YOU ARE IS A PARADISE FOR ME.

HONEY...

In 1946, Mandela's first son, Madiba Thembekile, was born.

NOW I HAVE A SON TO CARRY ON MY NAME. I HAVE FULFILLED MY RESPONSIBILITY TO MY FATHER'S TRIBE.

IS "THEMBI" TO BE HIS NICKNAME? HE IS SO CUTE.

THEMBI, GROW UP HEALTHY.

ISN'T HE? HE WILL BE A BEAUTIFUL PERSON.

THEMBI!
THEMBI!

HA, HA,
HA.

HE IS NOT ONLY
A FREEDOM FIGHTER
BUT ALSO A GREAT
FATHER.

In early 1947, Mandela stopped working for the law firm to focus his energy on studying. Mandela's family was living on Evelyn's small salary.

But, unfortunately, their first daughter, Makaziwe, died at nine months old from an unknown illness.

SOB

SOB

HE LOVES HIS KIDS
SO MUCH...

In 1948, the National Party, representing the white Afrikaners, won a surprise victory in the national election.

BREAKING NEWS!

THE NATIONAL PARTY WON THE ELECTION!

The National Party, led by Dr. Daniel Malan, promoted apartheid, a policy of apartness. The white residents of South Africa voted for the National Party because they felt threatened by the growing demand for equality between blacks and whites.

WE AFRIKANERS ARE SMARTER AND MORE POWERFUL THAN BLACK AFRICANS. WE WILL REMAIN THE ULTIMATE OWNERS OF THIS LAND!

CLAP! CLAP! CLAP!

THE NATIONAL PARTY OF SOUTH AFRICA!

WHY ARE THE AFRIKANERS MORE POWERFUL?

REMEMBER THAT THE AFRIKANERS ARE DESCENDENTS OF THE DUTCH WHO FIRST COLONIZED SOUTH AFRICA. THEIR LANGUAGE IS CALLED AFRIKAANS. THE MAJORITY OF SOUTH AFRICA'S WHITE POPULATION WAS AFRIKANER AND THE MINORITY WAS OF BRITISH DESCENT.

WHAT IS APARTHEID?

APARTHEID MEANS APARTNESS OR SEPARATION IN AFRIKAANS. THIS WAS A POLICY OF RACIAL SEGREGATION.

EVEN BEFORE 1948, SOUTH AFRICA'S LAWS ASSUMED THE SUPERIORITY OF WHITE PEOPLE. AFTER 1948, THE NATIONAL PARTY STRENGTHENED THE RACIAL SEGREGATION POLICY TO ALLOW THE WHITE MINORITY TO CONTROL THE BLACK MAJORITY.

I DON'T BELIEVE THIS. I NEVER EXPECTED THE NATIONAL PARTY TO WIN THE ELECTION.

HOW DO YOU THINK BLACKS WILL BE TREATED NOW?

ANC Youth League

As soon as they came to power, the National Party government introduced brutal new rules.

WE HAVE TO PROTECT THE PURITY OF SOUTH AFRICA. THEREFORE WE BAN MARRIAGE BETWEEN DIFFERENT RACES. PEOPLE ARE NOW ALLOWED TO MARRY ONLY THOSE OF THE SAME RACE.

In 1950, the government of South Africa introduced the Population Registration Act to label each person as either white, colored (mixed heritage), black, or Asian/Indian. The Group Area Act required different races to live in separate towns and neighborhoods.

May 1, 1950, Orlando West

The Communist Party and members of the Indian National Congress held a general strike, and thousands of workers did not go to their jobs.

FREE!

PROTECT OUR RIGHTS!

After this, the government passed the Suppression of Communism Act, to prevent people from forming groups to challenge the government. Breaking this law was punishable by death.

Suppression of Communism Act

The African National Congress criticized the government and demanded that blacks be given more civil rights.

But then, in 1951, Malan's government announced that most blacks could no longer vote. Black workers were limited to unskilled jobs, and they could work only in certain areas. The National Party also passed the Bantu Authorities Act to abolish the Native Representative Council, the only political council representing native Africans.

1952

Mandela, who had served as national president of the ANC youth league since 1951, also became an important leader in the ANC.

THE GOVERNMENT IGNORED OUR CLAIM TO CIVIL RIGHTS.

WE MUST DO SOMETHING TO SHOW THEM OUR POWER. LET'S JOIN WITH OTHER ORGANIZATIONS TO FORM A HUGE RESISTANCE MOVEMENT.

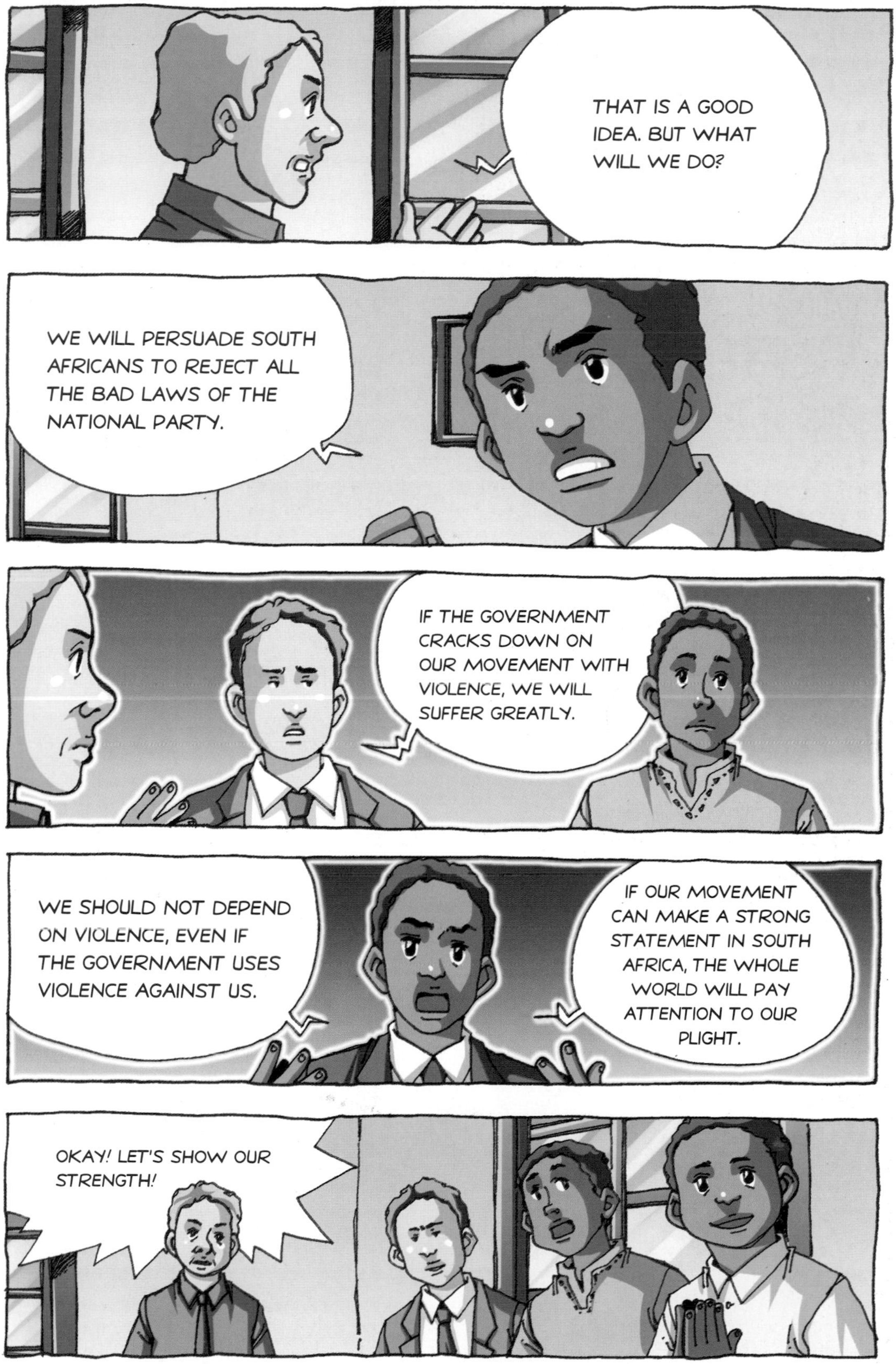
THAT IS A GOOD IDEA. BUT WHAT WILL WE DO?
WE WILL PERSUADE SOUTH AFRICANS TO REJECT ALL THE BAD LAWS OF THE NATIONAL PARTY.
IF THE GOVERNMENT CRACKS DOWN ON OUR MOVEMENT WITH VIOLENCE, WE WILL SUFFER GREATLY.
WE SHOULD NOT DEPEND ON VIOLENCE, EVEN IF THE GOVERNMENT USES VIOLENCE AGAINST US.
IF OUR MOVEMENT CAN MAKE A STRONG STATEMENT IN SOUTH AFRICA, THE WHOLE WORLD WILL PAY ATTENTION TO OUR PLIGHT.
OKAY! LET'S SHOW OUR STRENGTH!

Exit for white people at Port Elizabeth Station

On June 26, 1952, the ANC's Defiance Campaign officially began.

HEY, YOU! WHERE DO YOU THINK YOU ARE GOING? THIS EXIT IS FOR WHITE PEOPLE.

THIS IS OUR LAND. WHAT IS WRONG WITH WALKING ON OUR LAND?

GASP

YOU ARE BREAKING THE LAW!

WE DO NOT RECOGNIZE RACIST, UNJUST LAWS.

WE WANT OUR RIGHTS BACK! THIS IS OUR LAND, REGARDLESS OF OUR SKIN COLOR!

Across South Africa, black, Indian, and colored (mixed-heritage) protestors peacefully disobeyed the unjust laws.

NKOSI SIKELEL' IAFRIKA!

"Nkosi sikelel' iAfrika" was originally a Xhosa prayer and adapted as a national anthem in the 1800s. It was often sung by South Africa's oppressed peoples. For five months, 8,500 people joined the Defiance Campaign. They struggled bravely regardless of their job, age, and gender. They were not afraid to be sent to prison.

OPEN THE PRISON DOORS! ARREST US ALL!

END APARTHEID!

Mandela was so busy with his political activism that he spent less and less time with his family. Five-year-old Thembi and two-year-old Makgatho rarely saw their father.

YOUR FATHER COMES BACK HOME REALLY LATE. BUT HE ALWAYS KISSES YOUR CHEEK BEFORE HE GOES TO BED. YOU JUST DON'T NOTICE BECAUSE YOU ARE ASLEEP.

MOM, WHERE IS DADDY? I MISS HIM.

REALLY?

BUT— ...I STILL MISS HIM...

MY HUSBAND IS ALWAYS WORKING FOR OUR NATION, BUT HE DOESN'T LEAVE TIME FOR OUR FAMILY.

IAFRIKA, MAYIBUYE! (AFRICA, LET IT RETURN!)

In 1952, as thousands of people joined the resistance movement, Mandela and other ANC leaders were arrested.

WE CHARGE YOU WITH TREASON. YOU ARE SENTENCED TO 9 MONTHS OF LABOR AND TWO YEARS OF PROBATION.

The six months of nonviolent resistance against the government got many Africans involved in the political struggle. Thousands fought for their rights without fear of the police, courts, or prison.

WE HAVE YET TO ELIMINATE APARTHEID, BUT I AM SO PROUD OF OUR ORGANIZATIONS FOR CONTINUING THE PROTESTS FOR SIX MONTHS.

THIS IS JUST BEGINNING. I AM A FREEDOM FIGHTER NOW!

HURRAY FOR MANDELA!

EPISODE 6
THE STRUGGLE AGAINST APARTHEID

Annual meeting of the African National Congress, December 1952.

THE NATIONAL PARTY HAS BANNED ALL MEETINGS OF MORE THAN 10 AFRICANS AND THERE ARE NEW PUNISHMENTS FOR PROTESTORS. SOME RIOTS HAVE EVEN BROKEN OUT, AND WE DO NOT WANT TO USE VIOLENCE.

THAT'S GOOD!

AS YOU KNOW, NELSON MANDELA AND SOME OF OUR OTHER MEMBERS CANNOT ATTEND THIS ANNUAL MEETING.

THEY HAVE BEEN BANNED FROM ALL MEETINGS AND GATHERINGS.

Chief Albert John Lutuli was elected to lead the organization.

I AM HONORED TO BE THE PRESIDENT OF THE ANC. FREEDOM CAN BE ACHIEVED, EVEN IF WE MUST SUFFER.

HEY, NOW I REMEMBER! ALBERT JOHN LUTULI WON THE NOBEL PEACE PRIZE FOR HIS FIGHT AGAINST APARTHEID!

HOW DO YOU KNOW THAT?

I CAN DO RESEARCH TOO, YOU KNOW. HA, HA!

December 1952, Mandela and Tambo law firm

Mandela finally passed the examination and became a lawyer. He opened a law firm with his friend Oliver Tambo.

AS A LAWYER, I WANT TO HELP PROTECT THEM FROM UNJUST LAWS.

OKAY. I WILL HANDLE THE PAPERWORK AND RESEARCH. YOU CAN SPEAK IN COURT BECAUSE YOU ARE A GOOD SPEAKER. WE WILL MAKE FANTASTIC PARTNERS.

TAMBO, LOOK AT ALL OF THESE PEOPLE WHO NEED OUR HELP AND LEGAL REPRESENTATION.

THIS DISTRICT IS ONLY FOR THE OFFICES OF WHITE PEOPLE. YOU MUST MOVE YOUR OFFICE TO THE DISTRICT FOR BLACK PEOPLE.

NO, OUR OFFICE NEEDS TO BE IN THE CITY WHERE PEOPLE CAN FIND IT.

YOU BLACKS ARE NOT WELCOME HERE!

Mandela and Tambo kept their office in downtown Johannesburg and took on many cases of black Africans who had suffered under the new laws.

Meanwhile, the government passed even more apartheid legislation. Under the Pass Laws, black and colored Africans were required to carry a pass (stating their race, homeland, and occupation) at all times. They could not travel to other cities or areas without the pass.

The Reservation of Separate Amenities Act started in 1953. This law required people of different races to use separate public places, such as restaurants, buses, and parks.

NOW, IT'S LIKE HAVING TWO NATIONS WITHIN ONE NATION, AS THE LAW SEPARATES WHITE PEOPLE FROM BLACK PEOPLE EVEN IN PUBLIC PLACES.

MANDELA! HAVE YOU READ THE NEWSPAPER?

The Bantu Education Act was announced to govern black schooling.

NOT YET. WHY?

THEY WANT TO CONTROL THE SCHOOLS SO THAT BLACK CHILDREN WILL ONLY LEARN SKILLS FOR MANUAL LABOR. THIS WILL STOP BLACK CHILDREN FROM GETTING UNIVERSITY DEGREES OR BECOMING PROFESSIONALS.

I CAN'T BELIEVE THIS!

IF THEY DO NOT ALLOW CHILDREN TO LEARN, THEY WILL SOON MAKE SLAVES OF US ALL.

The African National Congress office

THIS ACT IS DESIGNED TO ERASE OUR FUTURE!

WE HAVE TO STAGE A DEMONSTRATION RIGHT NOW!

THE GOVERNMENT'S SUPPRESSION OF BLACKS HAS BECOME MORE SUBTLE AND SEVERE. I THINK THAT OUR FORMER NONVIOLENT ACTIVITIES, THE PROTESTS AND STRIKES, ARE NOT STRONG ENOUGH TO OPPOSE THE GOVERNMENT.

WE WILL HAVE TO FIGHT THEM.

BUT MANDELA, OTHER COUNTRIES ARE BEGINNING TO SUPPORT US IN OUR FIGHT AGAINST APARTHEID BECAUSE THEY SEE THAT WE USE NONVIOLENCE.

73

OUR PEACEFUL STRATEGY HIGHLIGHTS THE CRUELTY OF THE GOVERNMENT AND HELPS US TO GET SUPPORT FROM OTHER RACES. DO YOU UNDERSTAND?

YES, I UNDERSTAND THAT, AND I HOPE THAT NONVIOLENCE CAN CHANGE THE GOVERNMENT. HOWEVER, I AM NOT SURE THAT IT WILL WORK.

THIS PASSIVE RESISTANCE CAN'T BRING ABOUT A HUGE CHANGE. WE NEED STRONGER MEASURES.

Congress of the People conference at Kliptown, near Johannesburg, 1955

About 3,000 leaders from many African organizations attended the conference.

AT THE CONGRESS OF THE PEOPLE, THE ANC ADOPTED THE FREEDOM CHARTER.

ALL PEOPLE OF SOUTH AFRICA HAVE A RIGHT TO FREEDOM REGARDLESS OF THEIR RACE. WE VOW TO CONTINUE OUR STRUGGLE AGAINST RACISM UNTIL WE CAN BUILD A TRUE DEMOCRACY.

NKOSI SIKELEL' IAFRIKA!

HURRAY! YES!

December 5, 1956

BANG! BANG!

MANDELA, WE HAVE A WARRANT FOR YOUR ARREST. FOLLOW ME.

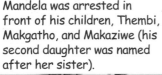

Mandela was arrested in front of his children, Thembi, Makgatho, and Makaziwe (his second daughter was named after her sister).

FATHER...

HONEY...

At the same time, more than 150 other activists were arrested for treason and plotting against the government.

IT'S GOOD TO SEE YOU AGAIN, FRIEND.

THANKS TO THE GOVERNMENT, WE CAN SEE EACH OTHER AGAIN. WE'VE BEEN BANNED FROM MEETING FOR SUCH A LONG TIME.

YOU'RE RIGHT. HA, HA!

Two weeks later, 156 activists were transferred to court for trials.

WE SUPPORT OUR LEADERS!

WE SUPPORT OUR LEADERS!

The government arrested the organizers of the Congress of the People. However, they were released on bail, for fear that their arrests would spark public riots.
However, the trial would still last for several years. They were kept under strict surveillance and had to be investigated by the police every week. They could not leave the towns where they lived.

SEE YOU AT THE NEXT TRIAL.

TAKE CARE!

MY CHILDREN WERE SHOCKED WHEN THEY WATCHED ME GET ARRESTED. I WILL CALM THEM DOWN.

THEMBI, MAKGATHO, MAKI! I AM HOME!

MANDELA, I CAN'T LIVE LIKE THIS ANY MORE. YOU MUST CHOOSE BETWEEN ME AND THAT CONGRESS!

I AM SO SORRY, EVELYN. BUT I HAVE NO OTHER OPTION.

FOR ME, BOTH ARE IMPORTANT. PLEASE UNDERSTAND.

Soon after, Evelyn left Mandela and they divorced. Thembi, who was 10 at the time, was shocked by his parents' divorce.

SOB

I WISH WE COULD EXPLAIN TO THEMBI HOW MUCH HIS FATHER LOVES HIM...

I KNOW. POOR THEMBI.

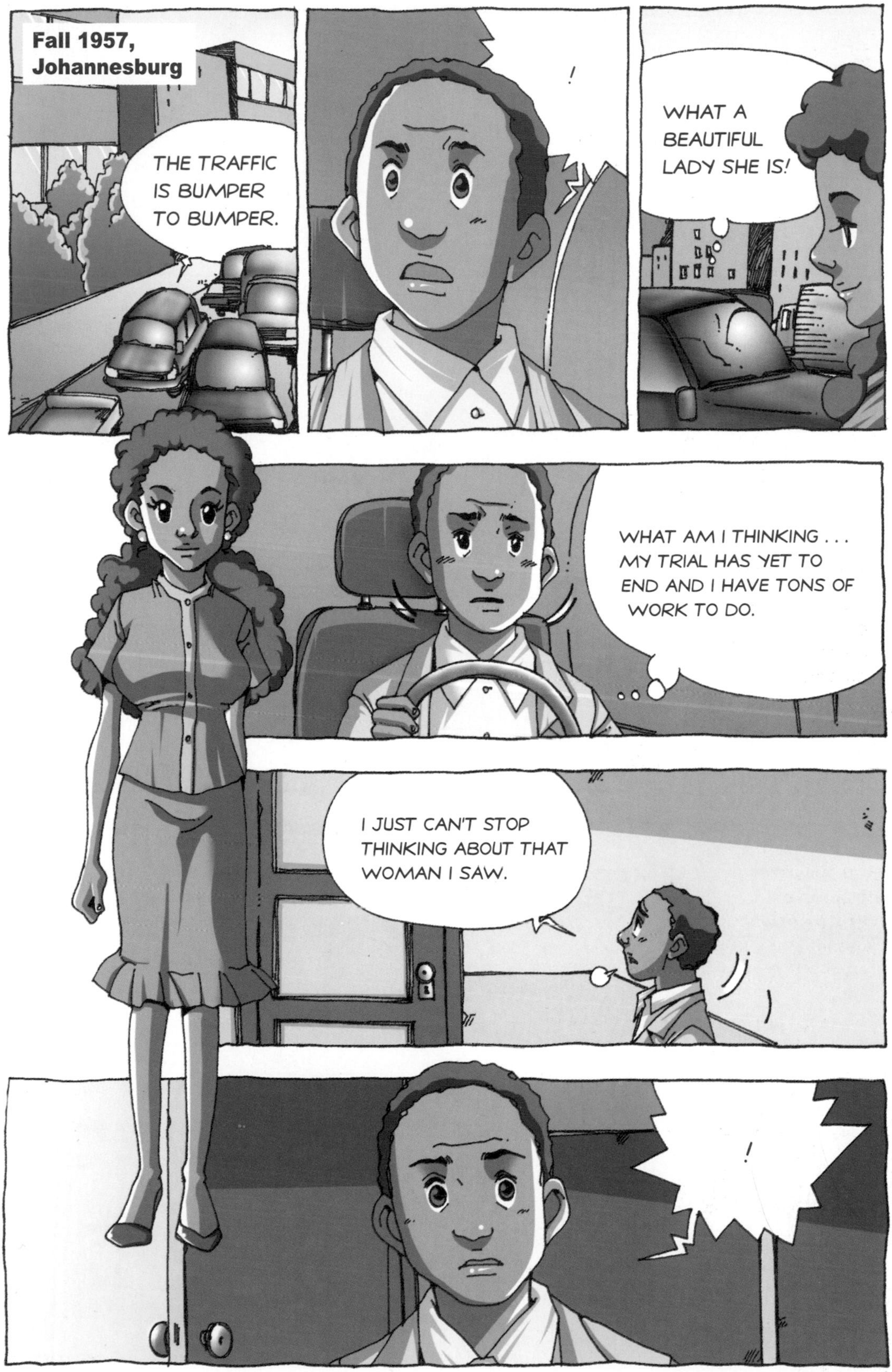
Fall 1957,
Johannesburg
THE TRAFFIC IS BUMPER TO BUMPER.
!
WHAT A BEAUTIFUL LADY SHE IS!
WHAT AM I THINKING . . . MY TRIAL HAS YET TO END AND I HAVE TONS OF WORK TO DO.
I JUST CAN'T STOP THINKING ABOUT THAT WOMAN I SAW.
!

OLIVER, WHO IS THAT WOMAN...?

SHE IS A SOCIAL WORKER AND SHE WANTS TO CONSULT US ABOUT LAW. HER NAME IS WINNIE.

Her South African name was Nomzamo Nobandla Winniefred Madikizela. In the Xhosa language, Nomzamo means a person who endures difficulties. Mandela and Winnie fell in love.

I LOVE YOU, WINNIE. I AM NOT RICH AND WE MIGHT NOT LIVE COMFORTABLY. BUT WOULD YOU MARRY ME?

YES, NELSON. I KNOW YOU HAVE A HARD AND BUSY LIFE WITH YOUR APARTHEID RESISTANCE WORK. I WANT TO BE YOUR PARTNER IN YOUR LIFE AND YOUR WORK.

They married on June 15, 1958. One year later, in February 1950, their first daughter, Zenani, was born.

In 1959, the National Party passed the Promotion of Bantu Self-Government Act. This act set up separate "homelands" as designated communities for black Africans that would have their own local governments. The aim was that these homelands would eventually become independent of South Africa.

Many people were angered. Robert Sobukwe, a former member of the ANC Youth League, started a new protest group called the Pan Africanist Congress (PAC). His group wanted to focus on the rights of black Africans, not Indians or coloreds. The Pan Africanist Congress organized protests to challenge the Pass Laws. One such protest was held in Sharpeville, a city near Johannesburg.

THEY WANT SOUTH AFRICA TO BE A WHITE NATION, SO THEY WILL PUT BLACK PEOPLE IN SEPARATE COMMUNITIES TO BE OUT OF THE WAY. BUT SOUTH AFRICA IS OUR NATION, TOO.

I HOPE THESE BLACKS DON'T RIOT.

WE DEMAND CIVIL FREEDOMS!

ABOLISH THE PASS LAWS!

THERE ARE ONLY 75 OF US. ON THE OTHER HAND, THERE ARE THOUSANDS OF BLACK PEOPLE PROTESTING OUT THERE. WE MIGHT GET KILLED.

BUT...BUT WE HAVE GUNS. I DON'T WANT TO DIE...

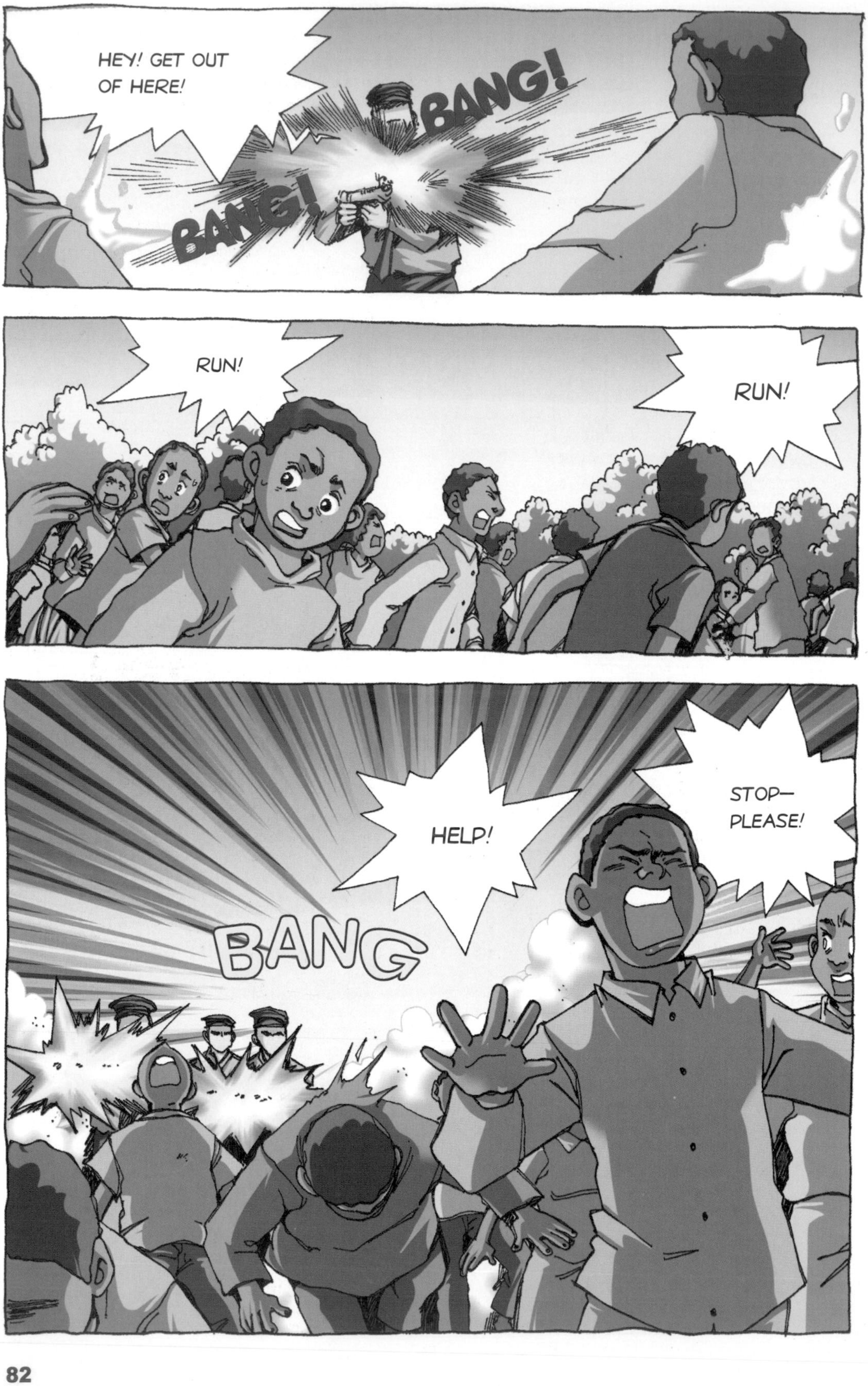
HEY! GET OUT OF HERE!
BANG!
BANG!
RUN!
RUN!
HELP!
STOP—PLEASE!
BANG

In the "Sharpeville massacre," 69 people were killed and more than 400 black protesters were injured. This event triggered demonstrations and riots across the nation. The international community blamed the government of South Africa for the incident.

African National Congress

CHIEF LUTULI, HERE ARE THE WAYS WE CAN RESPOND TO THIS CRISIS . . .

March 26, Pretoria

FELLOW AFRICANS . . .

LOOK AT THESE BURNING PASSES. THIS SYMBOLIZES MY WILLINGNESS TO FIGHT TO THE END, FOLLOWING THOSE WHO HAVE LOST THEIR LIVES IN THE MASSACRE.

I INVITE ALL OF YOU TO JOIN ME!

ABOLISH THE PASS LAWS!

WE WILL NEVER FORGET!

WE WILL FIGHT TO THE END!

LADIES AND GENTLEMEN, IN TWO DAYS, MARCH 26, WE WILL HAVE A DAY OF COMFORT AND REMEMBRANCE. DO NOT GO TO WORK, AND PAY TRIBUTE TO THE VICTIMS!

HURRAY!

HURRAY!

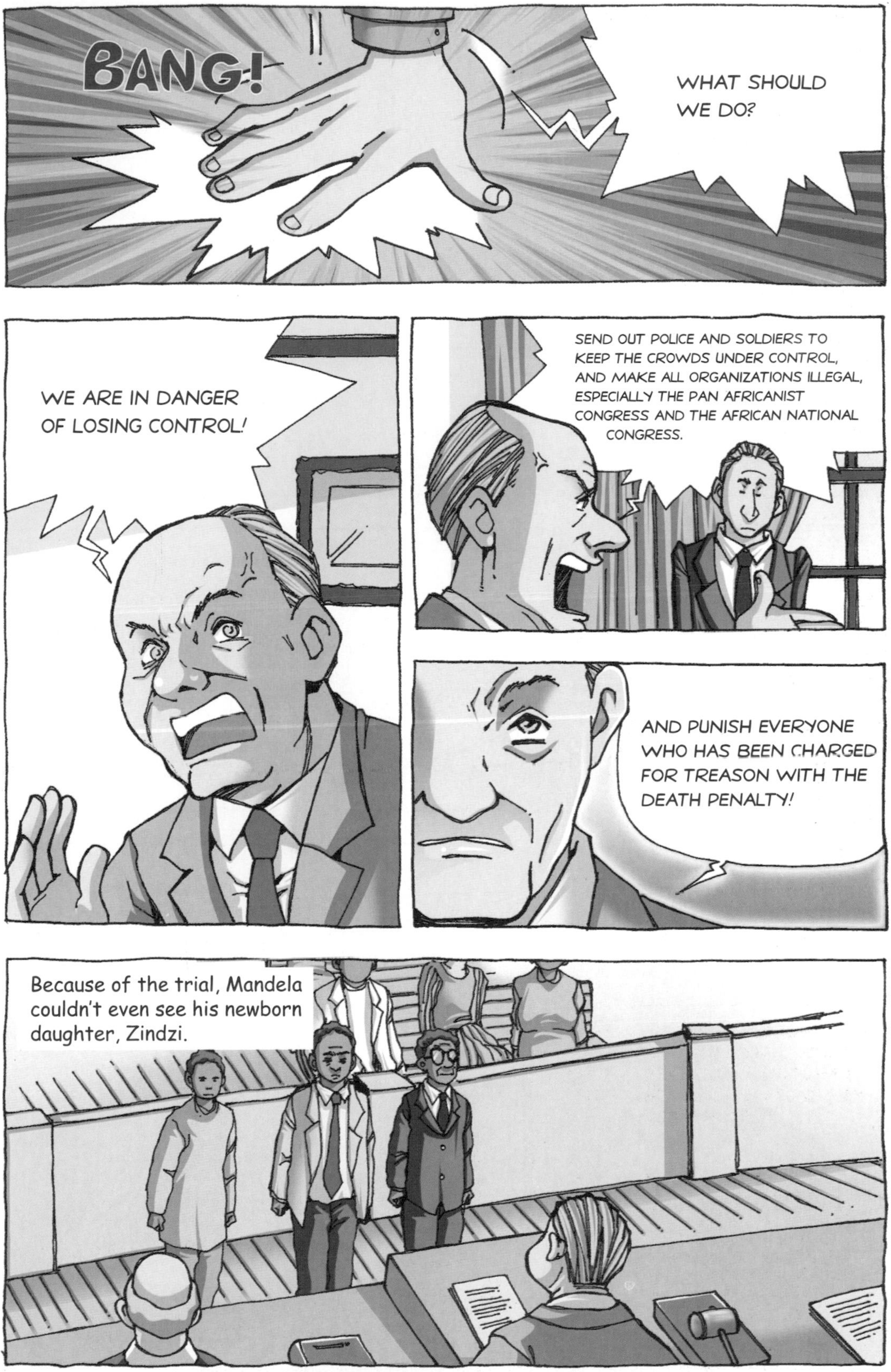
BANG!
WHAT SHOULD WE DO?
WE ARE IN DANGER OF LOSING CONTROL!
SEND OUT POLICE AND SOLDIERS TO KEEP THE CROWDS UNDER CONTROL, AND MAKE ALL ORGANIZATIONS ILLEGAL, ESPECIALLY THE PAN AFRICANIST CONGRESS AND THE AFRICAN NATIONAL CONGRESS.
AND PUNISH EVERYONE WHO HAS BEEN CHARGED FOR TREASON WITH THE DEATH PENALTY!
Because of the trial, Mandela couldn't even see his newborn daughter, Zindzi.

MANDELA, DO YOU KNOW HOW MUCH YOU HAVE HURT SOUTH AFRICAN SOCIETY?

YOUR HONOR, OUR ACTIVITIES WERE NONVIOLENT AND WE ONLY PROTESTED UNFAIR LAWS.

SIGH . . .

After five years, Mandela's "Treason Trial" finally ended.

IT IS TRUE THAT THE DEFENDANTS TRIED TO CHANGE THE GOVERNMENT. HOWEVER, WE CAN'T FIND ANY EVIDENCE THAT THEY PURSUED A VIOLENT COMMUNIST REVOLUTION.

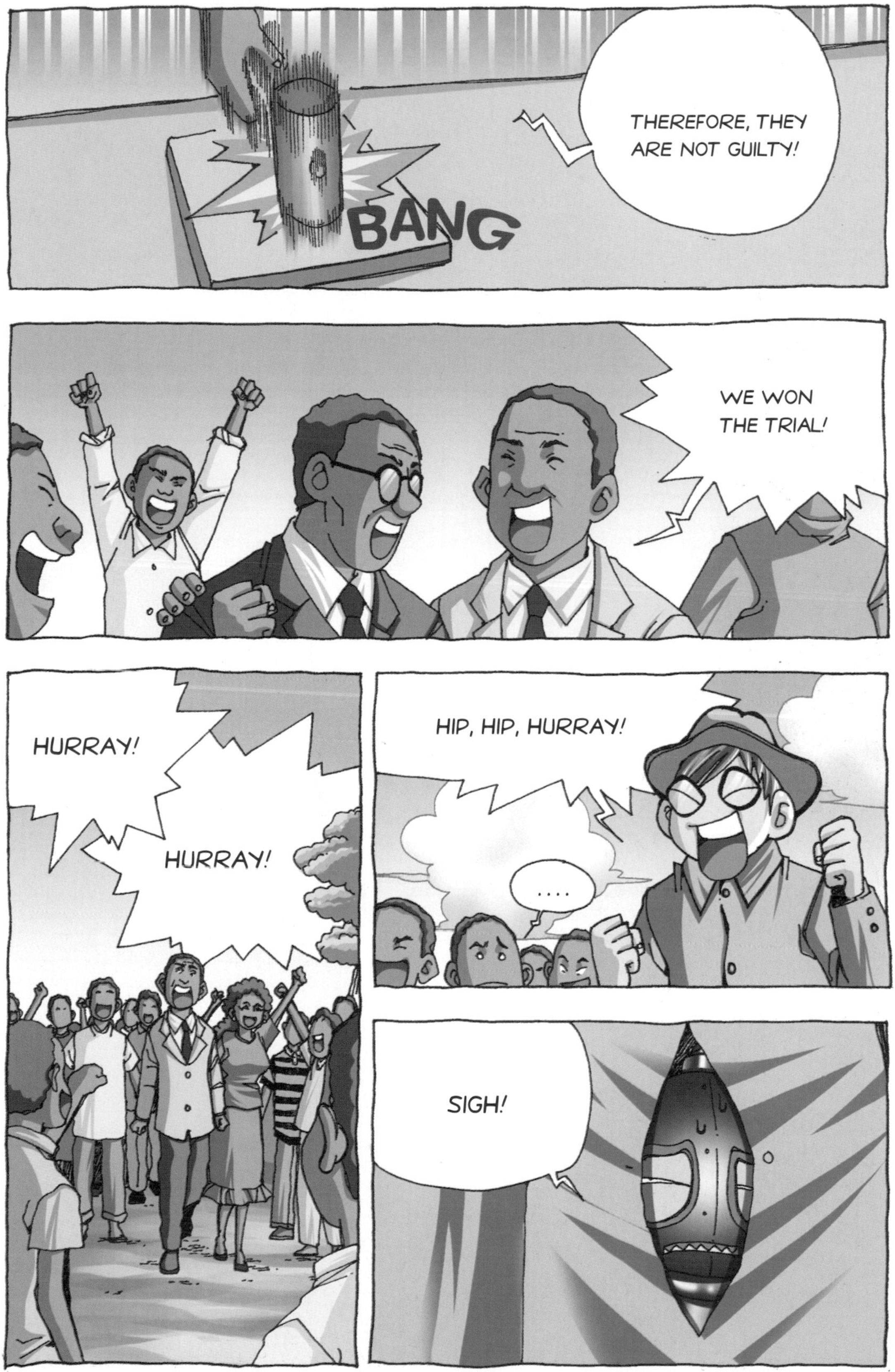
THEREFORE, THEY ARE NOT GUILTY!
BANG
WE WON THE TRIAL!
HURRAY!
HURRAY!
HIP, HIP, HURRAY!
....
SIGH!

EPISODE 7
THE SPEAR OF THE NATION

HOW ABOUT HAVING A DRINK TO CELEBRATE OUR VICTORY, MANDELA?

MAYBE I'LL HAVE A DRINK NEXT TIME, WALTER.

WHY?

WE WERE LUCKY THIS TIME. BUT I THINK WE ARE STILL IN DANGER, AND OUR COUNTRY STILL NEEDS MAJOR CHANGE.

THE COURT SAID THAT WE WERE NOT GUILTY. BUT OUR ORGANIZATION IS NOW AN ILLEGAL GROUP. WE MIGHT GET CAUGHT ANYWHERE AND ANYTIME.

NELSON, I AM SO HAPPY THAT YOUR TRIAL HAS FINALLY ENDED.

I'M SORRY, WINNIE. I DIDN'T WANT YOU TO SUFFER THIS.

NOW YOU SHOULD SPEND MORE TIME WITH ZENANI AND ZINDZISWA.

I WOULD LOVE TO, WINNIE.

After the trial, Mandela disappeared.

MANDELA, I KNEW YOU WERE EXTRAORDINARY THE FIRST TIME I MET YOU. BUT YOU SURPRISE EVEN ME.

As expected, Mandela was wanted by the police soon after the trial. He spent his days in hiding place and worked at night.

HE WASN'T FOLLOWED, WAS HE?

I THINK HE'S SAFE. HE'S VERY GOOD AT EVADING CAPTURE.

WHY DOES HE WANDER AROUND THE CITY? IT'S TOO DANGEROUS FOR HIM TO BE OUTSIDE OF HIS HIDING PLACE.

DID YOU HEAR THAT THE GOVERNMENT WITHDREW FROM THE BRITISH COMMONWEALTH AND IS ABOUT TO DECLARE SOUTH AFRICA A REPUBLIC?

YES. THE GOVERNMENT WANTS TO CONTROL THE NATION FREE FROM ENGLAND'S INTERVENTION, RIGHT?

SO MANDELA IS PREPARING A NATION-WIDE STRIKE.

OH, THAT'S WHY HE IS SO BUSY.

LET'S GET INSIDE.

WE WERE TOLD THAT MANDELA WILL BE HERE TONIGHT. INSPECT EVERYONE AND FIND HIM!

THAT WAS CLOSE.

DID YOU READ THE NEWSPAPER?

OF COURSE! I HAVE TO KNOW WHAT OUR GOVERNMENT IS UP TO.

UNDERCOVER POLICE OFFICERS TRIED TO ATTACK THE PLACE WHERE MANDELA HAS BEEN HIDING, BUT THEY COULDN'T CATCH HIM. I WAS REALLY HAPPY TO READ THAT NEWS.

MANDELA, OUR BLACK PIMPERNEL!

BLACK PIMPERNEL IS A WORD-PLAY ON SCARLET PIMPERNEL, A FAMOUS NOVEL BY BARONESS ORCZY. IN THE NOVEL, THE HERO CLEVERLY EVADES CAPTURE AS HE RESCUES INNOCENT PEOPLE FROM OPPRESSION AND PRISON.

I SEE. THAT IS A GOOD NICKNAME.

WHY DO THEY CALL MANDELA THE BLACK PIMPERNEL?

African National Congress

Mandela's strike lasted only three days before The protest was crushed by the government.

THE GOVERNMENT BRUTALLY SUPPRESSES OUR NONVIOLENT MOVEMENT AND REFUSES TO CHANGE ANY OF THESE TERRIBLE LAWS. I THINK IT'S TIME FOR US TO CHANGE OUR APPROACH.

MANDELA, I FIRMLY BELIEVE THAT NONVIOLENT MOVEMENT IS THE MOST EFFECTIVE WAY TO ACHIEVE OUR GOALS. WE DO NOT WANT TO KILL AND OPPRESS AS THE GOVERNMENT DOES.

WE CANNOT FEND OFF A WILD BEAST WITH ONLY OUR BARE HANDS!

THE CONGRESS CAN REMAIN A NONVIOLENT ORGANIZATION IF MANDELA ORGANIZES A NEW GROUP FOR ARMED BATTLE.

THAT'S AN IDEA!

THANK YOU FOR SUPPORTING ME. WE ARE WORKING FOR THE SAME GOAL, AND I WILL NEVER USE VIOLENCE TO KILL INNOCENT PEOPLE.

93

October 1961, Liliesleaf Farm, Rivonia

OUR ORGANIZATION WILL BE CALLED THE SPEAR OF THE NATION, OR MK. THE SPEAR MIGHT BE A SIMPLE WEAPON BUT OUR ANCESTORS USED IT FOR CENTURIES TO RESIST THE INVASION OF WHITE EUROPEANS.

NOW, WE HAVE TWO PRIORITIES.

SLOVO, WE NEED THE HELP FROM THE COMMUNIST PARTY. THEY CAN TEACH US HOW TO FIRE GUNS, MAKE BOMBS, AND WAGE A GUERRILLA WAR.

OKAY!

December 16, at a power plant in Durban

WALTER, WE NEED YOUR HELP TO RAISE THE MONEY FOR OUR WAR.

I KNOW.

WE ANNOUNCE THAT MK IS RESPONSIBLE FOR THE EXPLOSIONS IN JOHANNESBURG AND PORT ELIZABETH TODAY. WE DECLARE WAR ON THE GOVERNMENT. WE WILL FIGHT TO THE DEATH UNTIL WE ACHIEVE OUR FREEDOM.

SO THEIR ARMED STRUGGLE FINALLY BEGINS. IT'S IRONIC THAT AS SOON AS LUTULI RECEIVES THE NOBEL PEACE PRIZE, MANDELA'S SPEAR OF THE NATION STARTS A GUERRILLA WAR.

MANDELA! GOOD NEWS!

?

YOU WERE INVITED TO THE PAN AFRICAN FREEDOM MOVEMENT MEETING IN ETHIOPIA. TELL EVERYONE ABOUT SPEAR OF THE NATION, AND RAISE SOME FUNDS AND GET SOME WEAPONS FOR OUR WAR.

I WANT TO LEARN FROM THE NATIONS THAT HAVE BEEN LIBERATED BEFORE US. ALSO, I CAN MEET OLIVER, WHO IS LIVING IN EXILE.

MANDELA!

OLIVER TAMBO!

Accra Airport, Ghana

IT HAS BEEN TWO YEARS SINCE WE LAST MET. I BARELY RECOGNIZE YOU.

HAS IT BEEN TWO YEARS ALREADY? I HAVE BEEN BUSY OPENING BRANCH OFFICES OF THE AFRICAN NATIONAL CONGRESS AROUND THE WORLD.

Ethiopia

I ASK YOUR SUPPORT FOR THE SPEAR OF THE NATION, WHICH IS FIGHTING FOR A NEW AND BETTER FUTURE IN SOUTH AFRICA!

LOOK AT THEM. BLACK AND WHITE PEOPLE ARE SITTING TOGETHER, I WILL FIGHT UNTIL THAT HAPPENS IN MY COUNTRY.

Mandela met leaders of many other African nations to ask for their advice and support.

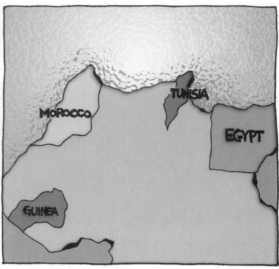

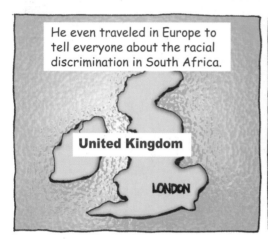

He even traveled in Europe to tell everyone about the racial discrimination in South Africa.

United Kingdom

LONDON

He went back to Ethiopia for war training.

ETHIOPIA

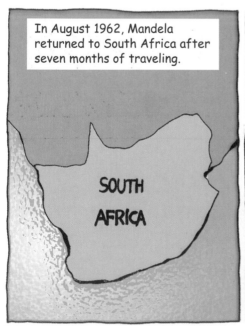

In August 1962, Mandela returned to South Africa after seven months of traveling.

SOUTH AFRICA

I MUST RETURN TO LEAD MK.

1962

But when he returned to South Africa, Mandela was arrested.

SCREECH

GASP!

MANDELA, YOU ARE UNDER ARREST FOR SABOTAGE, FOR STARTING STRIKES, AND FOR CONSPIRING AGAINST THE GOVERNMENT.

SNAP!

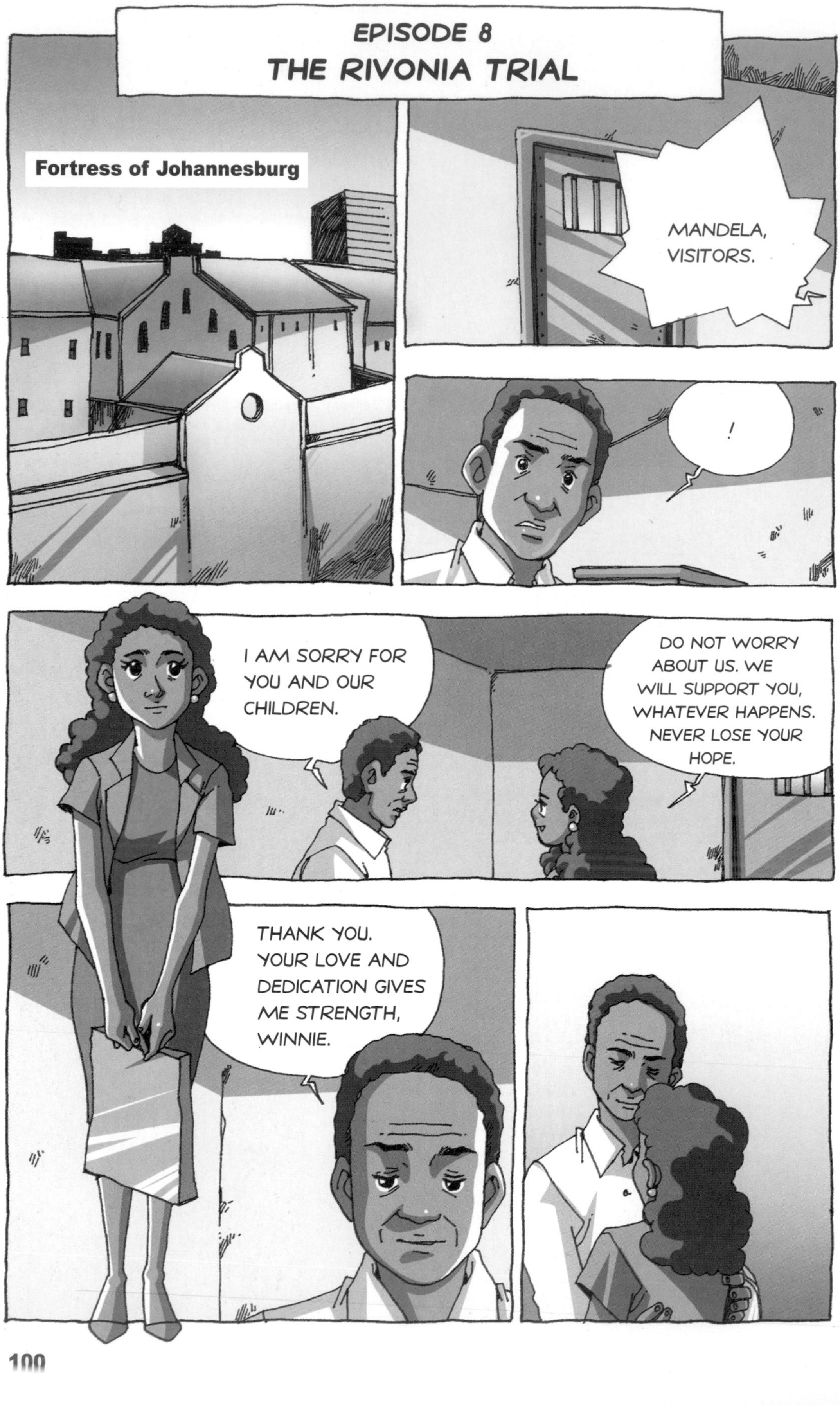
EPISODE 8
THE RIVONIA TRIAL
Fortress of Johannesburg
MANDELA, VISITORS.
!
I AM SORRY FOR YOU AND OUR CHILDREN.
DO NOT WORRY ABOUT US. WE WILL SUPPORT YOU, WHATEVER HAPPENS. NEVER LOSE YOUR HOPE.
THANK YOU. YOUR LOVE AND DEDICATION GIVES ME STRENGTH, WINNIE.

RELEASE MANDELA!

THE GOVERNMENT MUST RELEASE MANDELA!

The African National Congress started a "Release Mandela" committee and activism campaign.

I DON'T THINK THAT WE CAN WIN THIS TRIAL. WAIT UNTIL THINGS CALM DOWN AGAIN.

AMANDLA! POWER!

In October 1962, Mandela's trial was moved to Pretoria.

NGAWETHU! IT IS OURS!

Mandela defended himself at court.

I ADMIT ALL THE CHARGES AGAINST ME. BUT WHEN I FINISH MY TERM IN PRISON, I WILL CONTINUE MY STRUGGLE AGAINST APARTHEID.

THAT IS MY RESPONSIBILITY.

THE DEFENDANT IS SENTENCED TO THREE YEARS IN PRISON FOR STARTING A STRIKE AND ANOTHER TWO YEARS FOR TRAVELING ILLEGALLY. THAT WILL BE FIVE YEARS IN PRISON WITHOUT PAROLE.

OH, NO!

SOB...

July 1963, Liliesleaf Farm, Rivonia

GASP!

OWW!

LET'S SEARCH FOR CLUES.

By spying, the government found the headquarters of the MK. It made a sudden attack on the office to arrest all the members and seize evidence.

The Rivonia Trial

Nelson Mandela, already serving his term in prison, was again charged with sabotage as the leader of the Spear of the Nation.

MAYIBUYE IAFRIKA!

AMANDLA!

NGAWETHU!

THE DEFENDANTS ARE CHARGED WITH TREASON.

NELSON MANDELA. HOW DO YOU PLEAD?

YOUR HONOR, THE GOVERNMENT SHOULD BE ON TRIAL, NOT ME. I AM NOT GUILTY.

THIS IS THE HONORABLE COURT. JUST PLEAD GUILTY OR NOT GUILTY.

WALTER SISULU. HOW DO YOU PLEAD?

THE GOVERNMENT SHOULD BE BLAMED FOR THE CRIMES IN THE NATION. I AM NOT GUILTY.

The defendants refused to identify their attacks on the government as crimes.

HOW DO YOU PLEAD?

THE GOVERNMENT IS TO BE BLAMED. WE ARE DEFENDING THE PEOPLE OF SOUTH AFRICA.

The prosecutor had a witness who would testify against the accused.

LET ME CALL MY WITNESS. SIR, THIS WAY PLEASE.

THAT IS BRUNO MTOLO, THE HEAD OF NATAL'S BRANCH OF MK!

HE BETRAYED US!

THE SPEAR OF THE NATION IS LINKED TO THE COMMUNIST PARTY. IT RECEIVED HELP AND TRAINING IN HOW TO BOMB NATIONAL BUILDINGS FROM THE COMMUNIST PARTY.

HIS TESTIMONY HAS PUT US IN BIG TROUBLE. WE MIGHT BE SENTENCED TO DEATH.

I AM THE FIRST DEFENDANT, NELSON MANDELA.

Then the defense got their chance to speak.

FOR YEARS, THE AFRICAN NATIONAL CONGRESS HELD NONVIOLENT CAMPAIGNS TO END THE INHUMANE TREATMENT OF BLACKS BY THE GOVERNMENT. HOWEVER, THE BRUTAL LAWS CONTINUED. FINALLY, WITH NO OTHER CHOICE, WE DECIDED TO LAUNCH THE SPEAR OF THE NATION.

DURING MY LIFETIME, I HAVE DEDICATED MYSELF TO THE STRUGGLE OF THE AFRICAN PEOPLE. I HAVE FOUGHT AGAINST WHITE DOMINATION, AND I HAVE FOUGHT AGAINST BLACK DOMINATION. I HAVE CHERISHED THE IDEAL OF A DEMOCRATIC AND FREE SOCIETY IN WHICH ALL PEOPLE LIVE TOGETHER IN HARMONY AND WITH EQUAL OPPORTUNITIES.

IT IS AN IDEAL WHICH I HOPE TO LIVE FOR AND TO ACHIEVE. BUT IF NEED BE, IT IS AN IDEAL FOR WHICH I AM PREPARED TO DIE.

I WILL PREPARE FOR THE WORST.

SUCH A READINESS TO GIVE UP EVEN THEIR LIVES FOR WHAT THEY BELIEVE... I THINK I CAN UNDERSTAND WHY OUR PLANET MUD IS INFECTED WITH THE CONFUSION VIRUS.

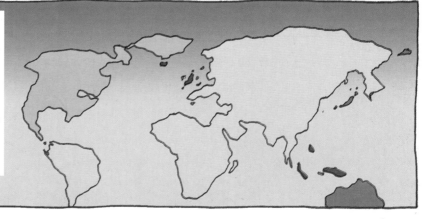

The world community paid close attention to the Rivonia Trial. The UN Security Council urged the government of South Africa to stop the trial and release the defendants.

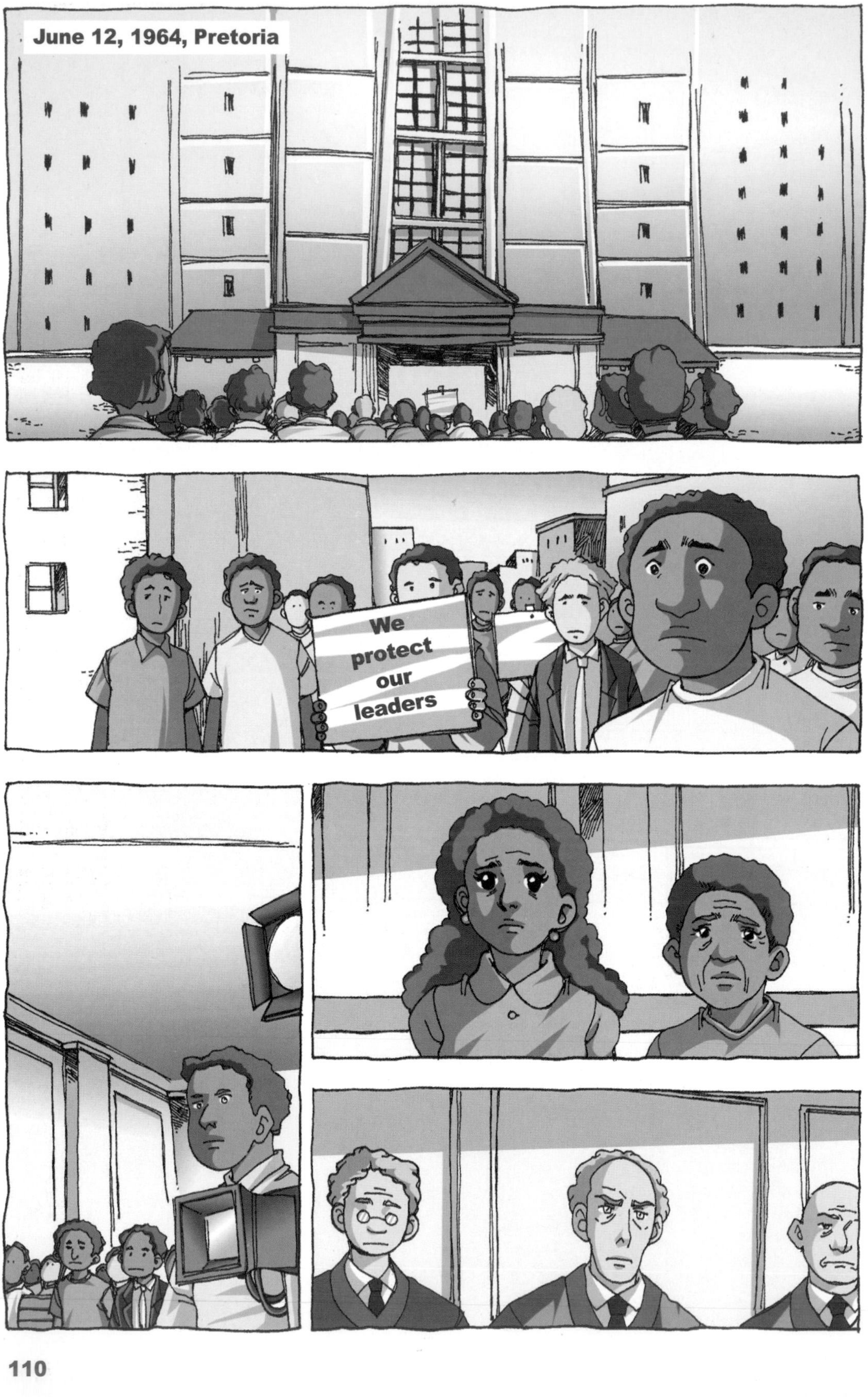
June 12, 1964, Pretoria
We protect our leaders

YOUR CRIMES ARE CONSIDERED TREASON. HOWEVER, AFTER CONSIDERING ALL THE FACTORS, THE COURT DECIDED NOT TO SENTENCE YOU TO THE DEATH PENALTY.

WE SENTENCE YOU TO LIFE IN PRISON.

BANG! BANG!

The eight leaders of MK, including Nelson Mandela and Walter Sisulu, were sentenced to life in prison.

AT LEAST IT'S NOT THE DEATH PENALTY!

THERE IS STILL HOPE!

THANK GOD!

AS LONG AS I AM ALIVE, I CAN CONTINUE THE MISSION, EVEN FROM PRISON!

EPISODE 9
ROBBEN ISLAND

Robben Island

MANDELA WILL BE DETAINED ON ROBBEN ISLAND.

IN DUTCH, ROBBEN MEANS SEAL. IT IS A VERY SMALL ISLAND NEAR CAPE TOWN. FOR CENTURIES, BLACK PEOPLE WHO RESISTED WHITE DOMINATION WERE IMPRISONED ON THE ISLAND.

THIS IS AN ISLAND OF SUFFERING AND INJUSTICE FOR BLACK PEOPLE.

THAT'S RIGHT.

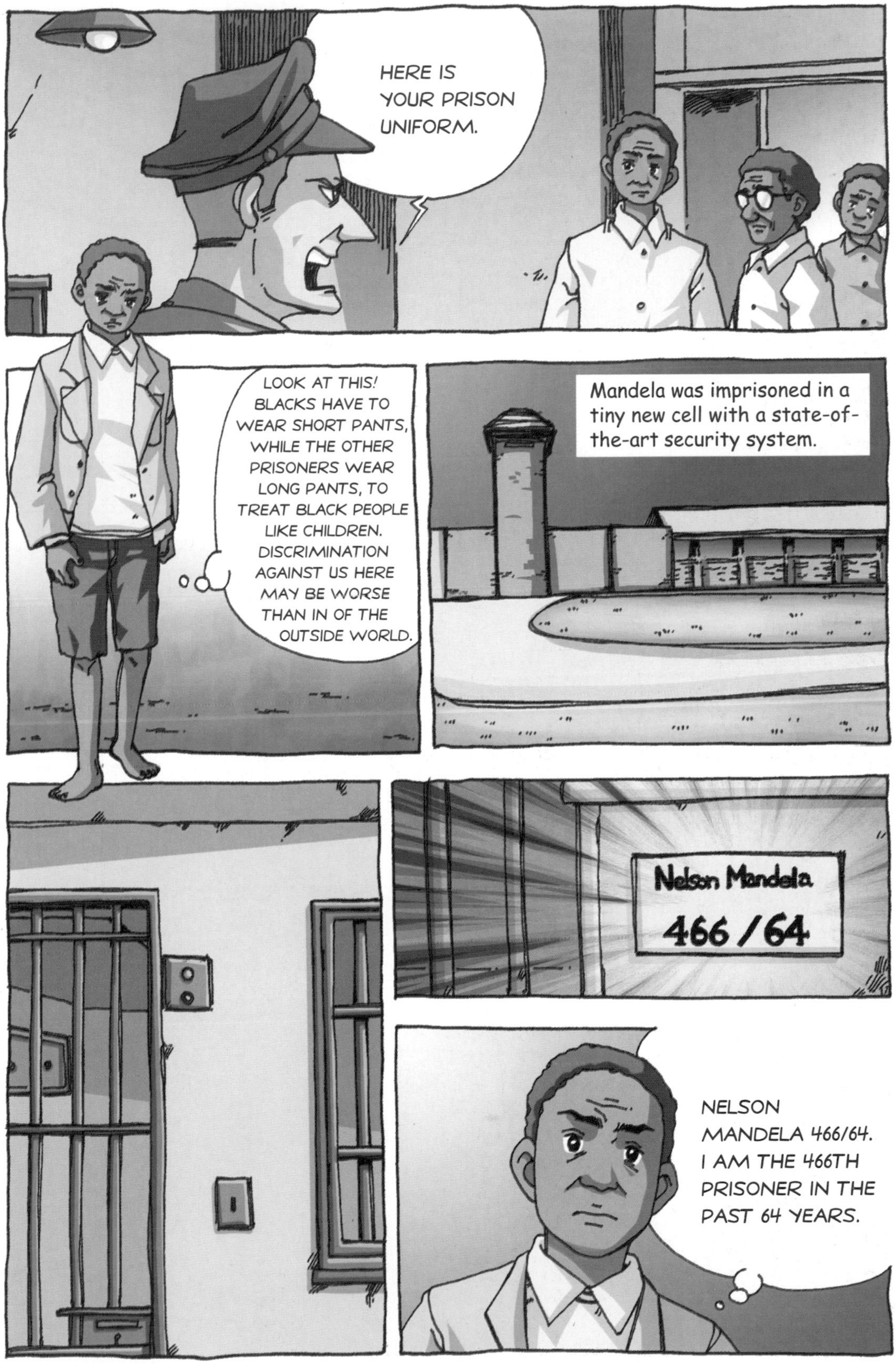
HERE IS YOUR PRISON UNIFORM.
LOOK AT THIS! BLACKS HAVE TO WEAR SHORT PANTS, WHILE THE OTHER PRISONERS WEAR LONG PANTS, TO TREAT BLACK PEOPLE LIKE CHILDREN. DISCRIMINATION AGAINST US HERE MAY BE WORSE THAN IN OF THE OUTSIDE WORLD.
Mandela was imprisoned in a tiny new cell with a state-of-the-art security system.
Nelson Mandela
466 / 64
NELSON MANDELA 466/64. I AM THE 466TH PRISONER IN THE PAST 64 YEARS.

MOVE!

BANG!

THIS IS MY HOME NOW.

IT IS HARD TO KEEP TRACK OF TIME IN PRISON. I SHOULD MAKE A CALENDAR SO I WON'T LOSE TRACK.

THIS PLACE DENIES OUR HUMAN DIGNITY. THEY WILL IGNORE AND CLAMP DOWN ON US TO MAKE US DESPAIR AND GIVE UP.

BUT I WILL NEVER GIVE UP, NO MATTER WHAT THE CIRCUMSTANCES. THAT LEADS ONLY TO FAILURE AND DEATH.

AT LEAST MANDELA WAS SENT TO THE SAME PRISON AS HIS FRIENDS. THAT WILL MAKE IT EASIER TO ENDURE LIFE IN PRISON, RIGHT?

I THINK SO.

The days in Robben Island were difficult to bear.

GET UP! QUICK!

QUICK! GET UP!

STOP EATING AND GET BACK TO YOUR WORK!

THIS IS NOT FIT FOR HUMANS.

YOU CAN'T KEEP UP YOUR STRENGTH UNLESS YOU EAT SOMETHING.

The days were long and boring.

WHEN CAN I SEE WINNIE? ALL I HAVE RECEIVED IS ONE LETTER OF GREETING FROM HER, BECAUSE THE GUARDS INSPECT ALL OF MY MAIL.

THEY ARE REALLY CRUEL. THEY CLASSIFY THE PRISONERS TO CONTROL US.

I AM IN THE LOWEST CLASS, D. THE PRISONERS OF CLASS D ARE ALLOWED TO HAVE ONLY ONE LETTER AND ONE MEETING IN SIX MONTHS. CLASS C PRISONERS ARE ALLOWED TO HAVE TWO LETTERS AND MEETINGS. MAYBE SOMEDAY THEY WILL UPGRADE MY LEVEL.

Three years after he was sent to Robben Island, Mandela was allowed to see Winnie.

FINALLY I WILL SEE MY WIFE AGAIN.

HONEY!

YOUR VISIT IS OVER!

30 MINUTES HAVE ALREADY PASSED?

I WILL COME AGAIN. TAKE CARE UNTIL THEN.

I HAVE TO ENDURE THE LIFE HERE. I HAVE TO BE STRONG FOR HER.

WINNIE MUST HAVE IT EVEN HARDER THAN I DO. HOW DIFFICULT IT MUST BE TO RAISE OUR TWO CHILDREN UNDER STRICT SURVEILLANCE AND OPPRESSION!

Mandela's first job in prison was breaking stones in the ground of the prison. Later, he had to dig limestone in a quarry.

GOSH, THIS IS TOO HARD. I MISS THE OLD WORK I DID BEFORE.

IF YOU THINK IT IS TOO HARD, YOU WON'T BE ABLE TO BEAR IT.

THE JOB MIGHT BE TOUGH, BUT I CAN SEE PLANTS AND TREES. WIND BLOWS HERE. AND I CAN WALK IN THE WOODS AND SMELL THE FLOWERS WHEN WE MOVE BETWEEN WORK AND THE PRISON.

MANDELA, WHAT ARE YOU THINKING? YOU LOOK DIFFERENT.

I USED TO BE SO ANGRY AND I FELT LIKE GOING MAD AT FIRST. BUT NOW I WANT TO ENJOY THE LIFE HERE AS MUCH AS I CAN BECAUSE I HAVE TO STAY HERE FOR A WHILE.

In the spring of 1968, Mandela was visited by his mother from Qunu, his sister Mable, and his grown-up son Makgatho and daughter Makaziwe.

MABLE, THANK YOU FOR BRINGING MOTHER HERE. MAKGATHO! MAKAZIWE! YOU ARE REALLY GROWN UP.

YOU ARE TOO THIN, MOTHER. YOU DON'T LOOK STRONG.

NO, I AM FINE. TAKE CARE OF YOURSELF.

SON, YOU WILL COME OUT OF THIS STRONGER THAN EVER. I HAVE ALWAYS BEEN PROUD OF YOU.

MOTHER...I AM WORRIED THAT I WILL NEVER SEE YOU AGAIN. PLEASE TAKE CARE.

TIME'S UP!

119

A few weeks later

OH, NO!

MY MOTHER HAS DIED?

PLEASE FORGIVE ME, MOTHER. I CAN'T EVEN ATTEND YOUR FUNERAL!

DID I MAKE THE RIGHT CHOICE TO SACRIFICE MY FAMILY FOR MY NATION? MY MOTHER WAS ALWAYS OPPOSED TO MY RESISTANCE ACTIVITIES AND MY FAMILY SUFFERS GREATLY.

NO, I MADE THE RIGHT DECISION. IN THE END, MOTHER TRUSTED AND SUPPORTED ME.

BUT SHE WAS ALSO PROUD OF ME FOR GOING ON A MISSION TO SAVE PLANET MUD.

HMM, I WONDER WHAT MY MOTHER IS DOING NOW? SHE WAS REALLY SAD WHEN I DECIDED TO TRAVEL TENS OF THOUSANDS OF LIGHT YEARS TO EARTH . . .

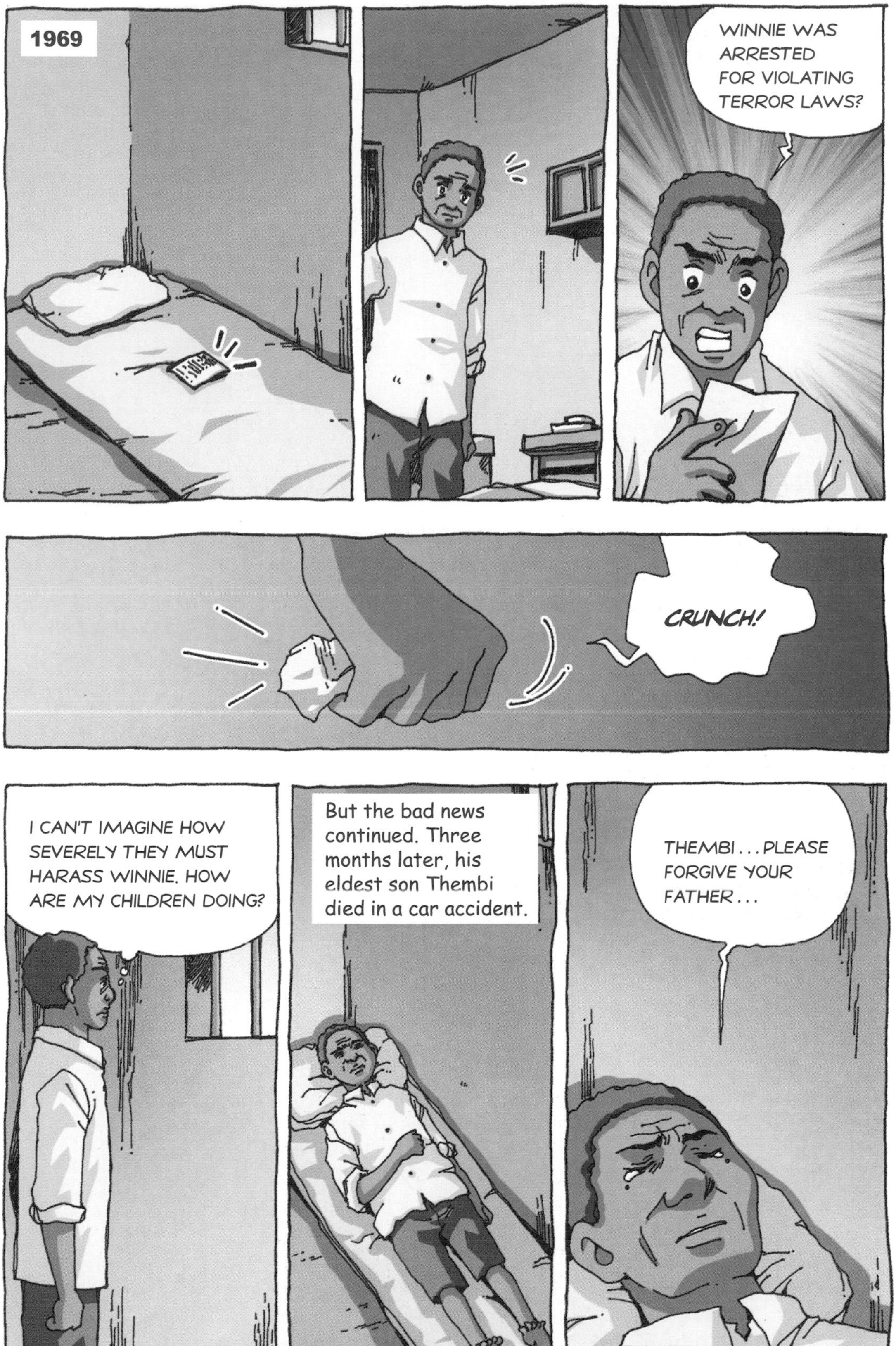
1969
WINNIE WAS ARRESTED FOR VIOLATING TERROR LAWS?
CRUNCH!
I CAN'T IMAGINE HOW SEVERELY THEY MUST HARASS WINNIE. HOW ARE MY CHILDREN DOING?
But the bad news continued. Three months later, his eldest son Thembi died in a car accident.
THEMBI . . . PLEASE FORGIVE YOUR FATHER . . .

A ray of hope was given to the dark life on Robben Island.

The black prisoners were finally given long trousers and better food.

IT'S GOOD TO WORK ON THE BEACH. ALL WE SAW BEFORE WERE ROCKS.

LOOK AT THE SEA, MANDELA. I FEEL RELIEVED NOW.

I FEEL LIKE I CAN REACH CAPE TOWN OVER THERE.

Soweto, South Africa, 1976

In 1974, a new law called the Afrikaans Medium Decree forced black schools to teach students English and Afrikans. This would put an end to the culture and languages of Africa's black people. In 1976, at a protest against this law in which thousands of black students and teachers participated, hundreds of protesters were killed, and over a thousand injured, by police.

RUN!

BANG!

BANG!

HELP!

The incident led to 16 months of riots in which 600 people were killed and 4,000 were injured. Most of the victims were young students. Thousands of young people were imprisoned. The Soweto riot shocked the world at South Africa's human rights violations.

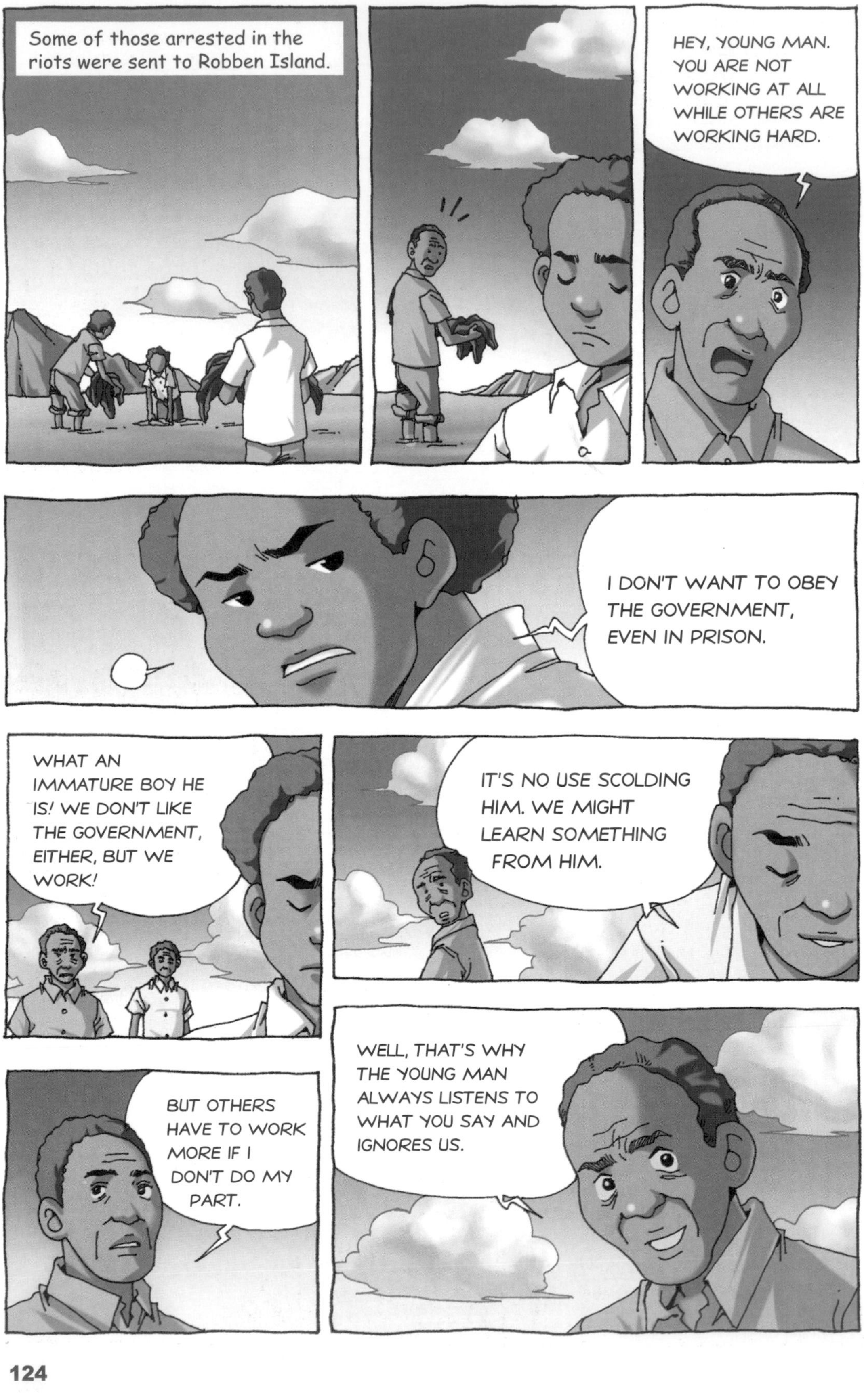
Some of those arrested in the riots were sent to Robben Island.
HEY, YOUNG MAN. YOU ARE NOT WORKING AT ALL WHILE OTHERS ARE WORKING HARD.
I DON'T WANT TO OBEY THE GOVERNMENT, EVEN IN PRISON.
WHAT AN IMMATURE BOY HE IS! WE DON'T LIKE THE GOVERNMENT, EITHER, BUT WE WORK!
IT'S NO USE SCOLDING HIM. WE MIGHT LEARN SOMETHING FROM HIM.
BUT OTHERS HAVE TO WORK MORE IF I DON'T DO MY PART.
WELL, THAT'S WHY THE YOUNG MAN ALWAYS LISTENS TO WHAT YOU SAY AND IGNORES US.

In 1977, forced prison labor ended on Robben Island.

NELSON, YOU DON'T HAVE TO WORK ANY MORE. WHY ARE YOU DOING THAT?

DOING NOTHING IS A PUNISHMENT HERE. I NEED SOMETHING TO CONCENTRATE MY ENERGY AND MIND. DON'T YOU AGREE?

WALTER, HOW ABOUT LEARNING HOW TO PLAY TENNIS WITH ME?

NO, THANKS. I LIKE TO STUDY.

In 1978, Mandela's daughter Zenani married Prince Thumbumuzi Dlamini, elder brother of King Mswati III of Swaziland. As a member by marriage of a reigning foreign dynasty, she was able to visit her father during his imprisonment.

YOU ARE PRECIOUS TO ME. THIS IS ONE OF THE MOST MEMORABLE MOMENTS IN MY LIFE.

FATHER!

I WILL NAME HER ZAZIWE, MEANING HOPE.

125

Although he was in prison for many years, Nelson Mandela was not forgotten by the people of South Africa. Instead, he was a burning hope for those who believed in his work against apartheid.

Mandela was given the Jawaharlal Nehru Award for his work against apartheid. On behalf of Mandela, his friend, the chair of the ANC, Oliver Tambo, accepted the prize.

The African National Congress led by Oliver Tambo held a major campaign to release Mandela and his colleagues. The Spear of the Nation continued to destroy important government buildings to urge the government to release them.

March 1982

GET PACKED YOU'RE BEING TRANSFERRED.

WHERE AM I GOING?

I CAN'T TELL.

WHERE ARE WE BEING TAKEN?

I FEEL LIKE I AM LEAVING MY HOME AFTER 18 YEARS IN THIS ISLAND.

WHERE ARE WE?

POLLSMOOR PRISON.

EPISODE 10
FREEDOM AND A FRESH START

Pollsmoor Prison was located in a beautiful suburban area of Cape Town.

WHY ARE WE HERE?

IT'S GOOD TO STAY TOGETHER. BUT I AM NERVOUS BECAUSE I DON'T KNOW WHY WE ARE HERE.

I'M SURE THEY WILL TELL US WHY WE ARE HERE AT POLLSMOOR PRISON.

May 1984

Something wonderful happened for Mandela. He was allowed to see his family.

MANDELA!

WINNIE!

IT HAS BEEN 21 YEARS SINCE I LAST HUGGED YOU.

THIS ANGEL MUST BE OUR YOUNGEST DAUGHTER, ZINDZI.

YES, FATHER!

I NEVER EXPECTED THIS! SO MUCH HAS CHANGED WHILE I HAVE BEEN IN PRISON!

The outside world had undergone major changes, too. Archbishop Desmond Tutu became the second South African to receive the Nobel Peace Prize for anti-apartheid work. The struggle in South Africa drew attention and support around the whole world.

Under pressure from the resistance movement, criticism from other countries, and economic restrictions, the South African government decided to compromise with Mandela.

I CANNOT ACCEPT THAT PROPOSAL.

PRESIDENT BOTTA SAID HE WOULD RELEASE YOU IF YOU PPROMISE TO UNCONDITIONALLY TO STOP USING VIOLENCE AND LIVE ONLY IN THE PLACES DESIGNATED FOR YOUR KIND.

The government told Mandela that if he promised to stop using violence against the government, they would let him out of prison. Mandela released a statement, and his daughter Zindziswa read the declaration on his behalf.

I LOVE FREEDOM AS MUCH AS YOU DO. HOWEVER, I DON'T WANT TO TRADE MY FREEDOMS FOR THOSE OF OTHERS. I WILL FIGHT UNTIL WE ALL OBTAIN OUR FREEDOM. I REFUSE THE GOVERNMENT'S OFFER, AND I WILL STAY IN PRISON UNTIL WE ACHIEVE OUR GOAL.

HURRAY!

MANDELA! MANDELA!

Mandela refused the conditional release and decided to remain in prison. However, he continued to negotiate with the government.

I AM WILLING TO CONVERSE AND COOPERATE WITH YOUR GOVERNMENT. PLEASE LET ME HAVE A MEETING WITH THE PRESIDENT.

I SEE. I WILL DELIVER YOUR MESSAGE TO THE PRESIDENT.

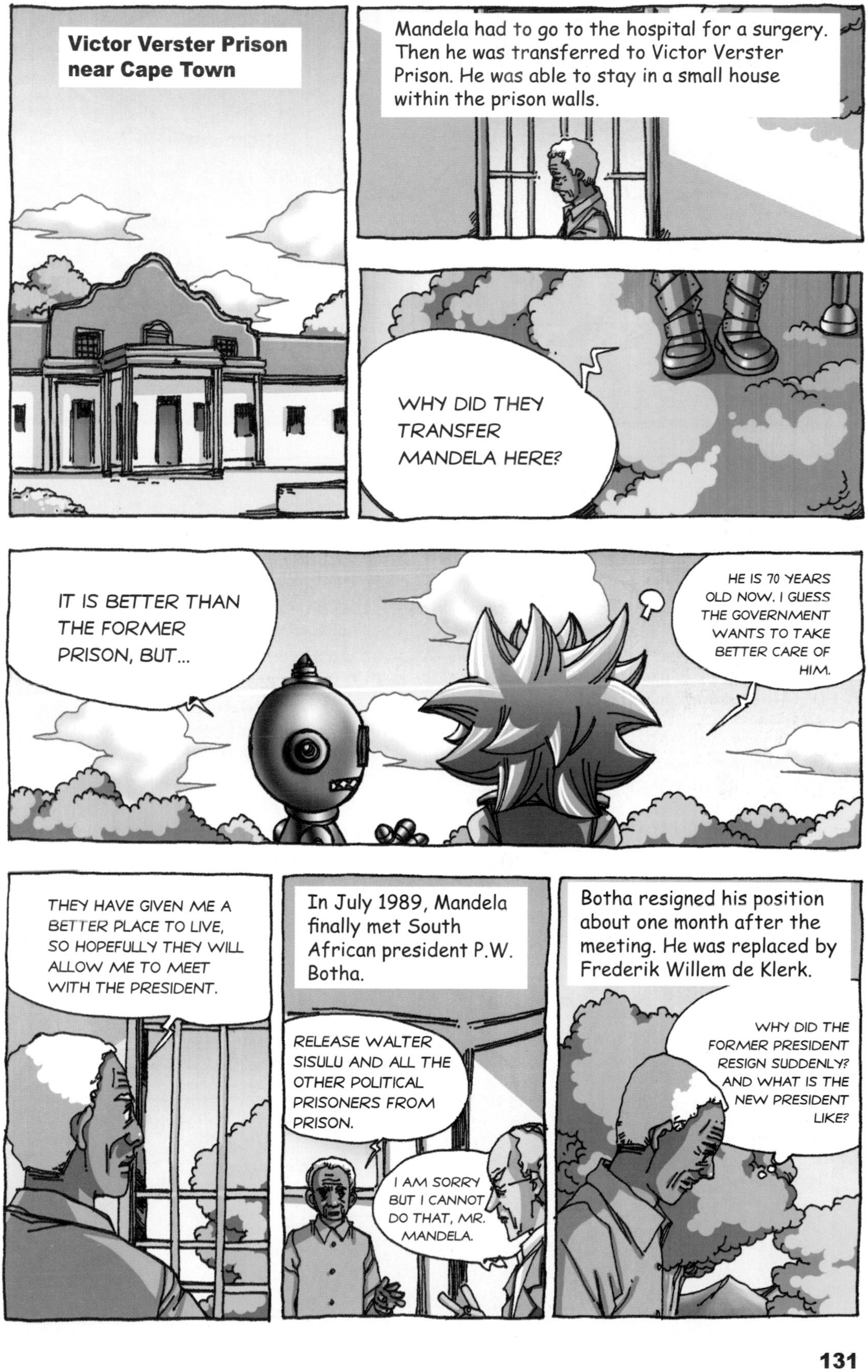

Victor Verster Prison near Cape Town
Mandela had to go to the hospital for a surgery. Then he was transferred to Victor Verster Prison. He was able to stay in a small house within the prison walls.
WHY DID THEY TRANSFER MANDELA HERE?
IT IS BETTER THAN THE FORMER PRISON, BUT...
HE IS 70 YEARS OLD NOW. I GUESS THE GOVERNMENT WANTS TO TAKE BETTER CARE OF HIM.
THEY HAVE GIVEN ME A BETTER PLACE TO LIVE, SO HOPEFULLY THEY WILL ALLOW ME TO MEET WITH THE PRESIDENT.
In July 1989, Mandela finally met South African president P.W. Botha.
RELEASE WALTER SISULU AND ALL THE OTHER POLITICAL PRISONERS FROM PRISON.
I AM SORRY BUT I CANNOT DO THAT, MR. MANDELA.
Botha resigned his position about one month after the meeting. He was replaced by Frederik Willem de Klerk.
WHY DID THE FORMER PRESIDENT RESIGN SUDDENLY? AND WHAT IS THE NEW PRESIDENT LIKE?

I GUESS HE HAS A LOT TO THINK ABOUT. HE JUST STARTED IMPORTANT NEGOTIATIONS WITH THE PRESIDENT.

WHAT CAN YOU TELL ME ABOUT PRESIDENT DE CLERK?

F.W. de Klerk was born in Johannesburg in 1936. He came from a conservative family that accepted South Africa's apartheid policies. He started his career as a lawyer. In 1972, he became a member of the National Party. He served as Secretary of the Interior, Education Minister, and in other important jobs.

I WILL WRITE A LETTER TO HIM TO FIND OUT WHAT HE IS LIKE.

In October 1989, de Klerk's government released Walter Sisulu and other political prisoners.

I CAN'T BELIEVE WE ARE FINALLY RELEASED!

IT'S GOOD TO BREATHE THE AIR OF FREEDOM!

December 1989, Victor Verster Prison

YOU WANT A FRESH START FOR SOUTH AFRICA, SO FIRST YOU MUST PUT AN END TO RACIAL DISCRIMINATION. RACIAL DISCRIMINATION IS THE CAUSE OF MANY PROBLEMS WE ARE SUFFERING NOW.

Mandela and President de Klerk had their first meeting.

IS THAT RIGHT?

YOU LISTEN WITH AN OPEN MIND. I THINK WE CAN WORK TOGETHER.

Parliament, February 2, 1990

I, PRESIDENT F.W. DE KLERK, ANNOUNCE THAT ALL BLACK AFRICAN ORGANIZATIONS, INCLUDING THE AFRICAN NATIONAL CONGRESS, ARE LEGAL ONCE AGAIN. FURTHERMORE, WE WILL RELEASE ALL POLITICAL PRISONERS AND ABOLISH THE DEATH PENALTY.

WE WANT TO SEEK TRUE PEACE IN THE REPUBLIC OF SOUTH AFRICA.

WHAT?

DID I HEAR THAT RIGHT?

Victor Verster Prison

YOU WILL BE RELEASED TOMORROW. WE WILL TAKE YOU TO JOHANNESBURG AND RELEASE YOU OFFICIALLY THERE.

TOMORROW?

AFTER SO MANY YEARS OF WAITING AND HOPING, NOW IT'S HAPPENING SO FAST! I WANT TO BE RELEASED ONE WEEK LATER FROM HERE, VICTOR VERSTER PRISON.

OKAY, MR. MANDELA. YOU CAN BE RELEASED FROM VICTOR VERSTER PRISON. BUT, WE CAN'T CHANGE THE DATE, BECAUSE WE HAVE ALREADY ANNOUNCED THE NEWS.

February 11, 1990

TIME, WHICH STOPPED IN PRISON, STARTS TICKING AGAIN. SOUTH AFRICA WILL SEE MANY CHANGES. I WILL DO MY BEST TO HELP THE COUNTRY CHANGE.

SHALL WE GO?

Mandela, who was 71 years old, was about to start a new life after spending 10,000 days in prison.

MANDELA! MANDELA!

HURRAY!

HURRAY FOR MANDELA!

President de Klerk did away with many policies central to apartheid, including the Native Land Act, the Group Areas Act, the Reservation of Separate Amenities Act, and the Population Registration Act. Ending these laws helped to restore some of the rights of black Africans and signified that apartheid would end soon.

MAYIBUYE IAFRIKA!

WE WILL HAVE FREEDOM AND EQUALITY!

OLIVER, I AM SORRY THAT YOU ARE NOT FEELING STRONG.

DON'T WORRY, I AM FINE.

Mandela met Oliver Tambo, who had finally come home after his long exile. But he was very ill.

I AM GLAD TO SEE YOU BECOME THE CHAIR OF THE AFRICAN NATIONAL CONGRESS.

TRULY, I AM GRATEFUL THAT MANY PEOPLE TRUST ME. BUT I AM WORRIED THAT I CAN'T MANAGE MANY MORE JOBS AT THE SAME TIME.

SOON, I WILL HOLD A MEETING THAT ALL LEADERS, REGARDLESS OF THEIR SKIN COLOR, CAN ATTEND, TO DISCUSS THE FUTURE OF THIS NATION.

IT IS NOT AN EASY TASK. BUT I FIRMLY BELIEVE THAT WE CAN BEGIN A NEW ERA IN SOUTH AFRICAN HISTORY IF WE CONTINUE OUR EFFORTS.

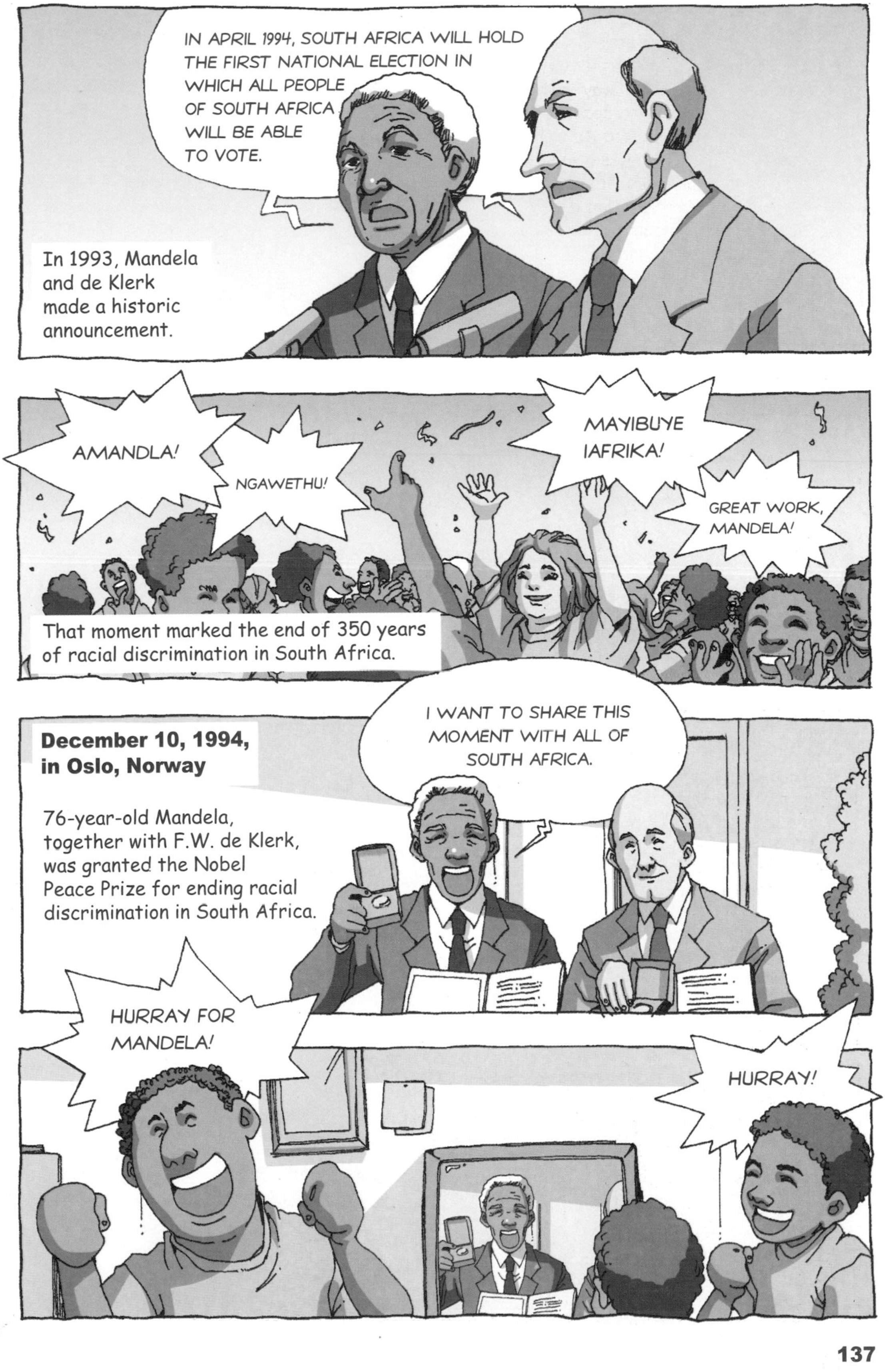
IN APRIL 1994, SOUTH AFRICA WILL HOLD THE FIRST NATIONAL ELECTION IN WHICH ALL PEOPLE OF SOUTH AFRICA WILL BE ABLE TO VOTE.
In 1993, Mandela and de Klerk made a historic announcement.
AMANDLA!
NGAWETHU!
MAYIBUYE IAFRIKA!
GREAT WORK, MANDELA!
That moment marked the end of 350 years of racial discrimination in South Africa.
December 10, 1994, in Oslo, Norway
I WANT TO SHARE THIS MOMENT WITH ALL OF SOUTH AFRICA.
76-year-old Mandela, together with F.W. de Klerk, was granted the Nobel Peace Prize for ending racial discrimination in South Africa.
HURRAY FOR MANDELA!
HURRAY!

In April 1994, the historic election was held.

MR. MANDELA, WHO ARE YOU GOING TO VOTE FOR?

I WILL WORRY ABOUT IT IN THE MORNING.

The African National Congress Center

HURRAY!

The African National Congress became the ruling party with 62% of votes in the election.

WE WON THE ELECTION!

FINALLY, OUR VOTES CAN MAKE A DIFFERENCE!

Nelson Mandela became the first black president of South Africa.

AMANDLA!

NGAWETHU!

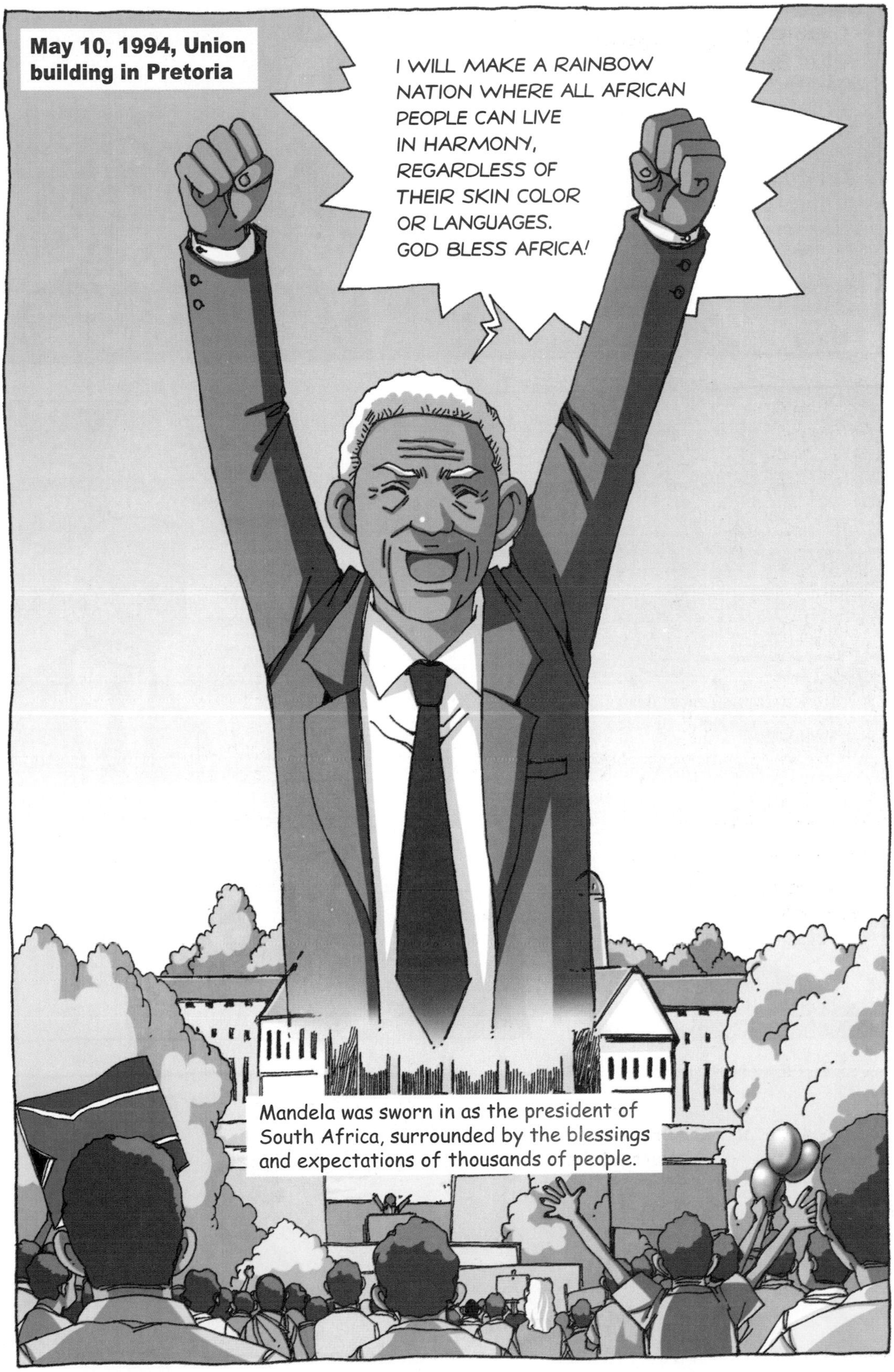
May 10, 1994, Union building in Pretoria
I WILL MAKE A RAINBOW NATION WHERE ALL AFRICAN PEOPLE CAN LIVE IN HARMONY, REGARDLESS OF THEIR SKIN COLOR OR LANGUAGES. GOD BLESS AFRICA!
Mandela was sworn in as the president of South Africa, surrounded by the blessings and expectations of thousands of people.

Thabo Mbeki, son of Mandela's colleague Govan Mbeki, became the first vice president, and de Klerk the second, of the parliament.

In 1995, President Mandela appointed Archbishop Tutu to lead the Truth and Reconciliation Commission to investigate human rights violations during the apartheid period.

WE CAN FORGIVE WHAT HAS BEEN DONE IN THE PAST. HOWEVER, WE SHOULD NOT FORGET OUR PAST. TRUE PEACE CAN HAPPEN ONLY WHEN THE TRUTH IS REVEALED.

IT WILL HELP US TO RECOVER FROM OUR SAD HISTORY AS PEOPLE ADMIT THEIR WRONGDOINGS AND VICTIMS SHARE THEIR EXPERIENCES.

The Truth and Reconciliation Commission investigated not only wrongdoings of white people but also human rights violations by black people. Even leaders of the African National Congress were investigated.

Mandela worked to remedy the poverty of South Africa's black people while trying to reconcile whites and blacks. However, he couldn't fix poverty overnight.

I HAVE DONE WHAT I COULD FOR SOUTH AFRICA. NOW THIS NEW NATION NEEDS A YOUNG LEADER.

I AM NOT WORRIED ABOUT HANDING OVER THE PRESIDENCY AT THIS HARD TIME, MBEKI. I BELIEVE YOU WILL LEAD THE NATION IN THE RIGHT DIRECTION.

I WILL DO MY BEST.

Mandela quit his job as chair of the African National Congress in 1997 and gave up the presidency in 1999.

WHAT ARE YOU GOING TO DO AFTER YOU RETIRE?

I WILL RETURN TO MY HOMETOWN, QUNU, WHERE MY MOTHER WAS BURIED.

FINALLY I RETURN TO MY CHILDHOOD HOME!

HE COULD CONTINUE HIS PRESIDENCY IN SOUTH AFRICA IF HE WANTED TO. PEOPLE LOVE MANDELA BECAUSE HE IS MODEST AND WISE.

Town of Qunu

Mandela settled down in Qunu with his new wife Graca Machel, widow of the former Mozambican president. He had divorced Winnie for her controversial political activities. He remarried on his 80th birthday.

However, Mandela was a revered leader throughout the world. Many needed his help and he went whenever he was needed.

He built a foundation to help African children dying from starvation or AIDS. He was also appointed as a peacekeeper in Rwanda/Burundi, a site of civil war.

Mandela's efforts to promote peace and stability in Africa and around the world will continue until his life ends.

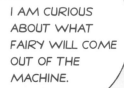

NELSON MANDELA WAS A REALLY GREAT PERSON.

I AM CURIOUS ABOUT WHAT FAIRY WILL COME OUT OF THE MACHINE.

HISS

BANG! CLUNK!

HEY!

When the brown dust from the "determination fairy,"–which gets its powers from Nelson Mandela's faith and courage, is sprayed on you, you will gain the determination to finish what you have put your mind to.

The effects double when it is used together with Gandhi's courage fairy.

WE COMPLETED THIS MISSION!

LET'S GO!

LET'S GO BACK HOME TO PLANET MUD.

I CAN'T WAIT!

❥ Nelson Mandela was awarded the Nobel Peace Prize in 1993. The prize was shared with former South African President F. W. de Clerk, the man who released Mandela from prison.

❥ Mandela's love for children inspired him to develop the Nelson Mandela Children's Fund in 1994. The foundation sets up programs throughout South Africa to aid children who have been abandoned, abused, or affected by poverty, HIV/AIDS, deafness, or other problems. Mandela's foundation also promotes leadership, the arts, and children's rights.

❥ Nelson Mandela has received many awards recognizing his contributions to reconciliation and world peace and honoring his stands for justice and peace while emphasizing understanding and harmony.

❥ UNICEF and the Hamburg Society for the Promotion of Democracy and International Law teamed with the Nelson Mandela Foundation to develop the Schools for Africa Project. The program is working to establish schools in six African countries where children currently do not have access to public education.

♦ Mandela was named *Time* magazine's Man of the Year in 1993 and was chosen as one of *Time's* 100 Most Important People of the Century in the Leaders and Revolutionaries category in 1998.

Fun Fact — *Never Let Them See You Sweat*

Mandela and a friend, Richard, were flying across Africa on a small plane when the pilot made a terrifying discovery—one of the plane's propellers had stopped. Mandela remained calm while a panicked Richard rushed to the cockpit. When Richard returned, he gave Mandela the news—ambulances were on stand-by at the airport and the runways were being coated with foam in case of a crash landing. Mandela took the news in stride and simply went back to reading his newspaper. Richard was amazed that Mandela could be so relaxed in such a desperate situation.

Later, when they had avoided a disaster and landed safely, Mandela admitted to Richard that he had really been scared when they were on the plane. Richard was surprised. Mandela had seemed so calm. Richard marveled at Mandela's remarkable strength. Then he realized that "Courage is being terrified and not showing it." Mandela demonstrated that courage not just only on the plane that day, but throughout his entire life.

When	What
1910s–20s	**1918** Rolihlahla (Nelson) Mandela is born in South Africa **1919** Following WW,I the first international peace organization, the League of Nations, is formed **1922** Egypt gains its independence from Britain **1922** The tomb of Egyptian king Tutankhamen is discovered **1927** Mandela's father dies; he is raised by the Thembu chief Jongintaba
1930s	**1936** Italy controls Ethiopia **1939** South Africa enters World War II **1939** Mandela enrolls at Fort Hare University
1940s	**1941** The Japanese attack Pearl Harbor, and the United States enters WWII **1943** Mandela joins the African National Congress (ANC) as an activist **1944** Mandela and others create the ANC Youth League **1945** Fifty-one nations create the United Nations international peacekeeping organization **1946** India gains independence from Britain and splits into India and Pakistan **1948** The National Party comes to power in South Africa and aggressive apartheid policies begin **1949** The ANC Youth League organizes movement strikes, boycotts, protests, and passive resistance against the apartheid policies
1950s	**1951** Mandela becomes national president of the ANC Youth League **1952** The ANC starts the Defiance Campaign, a nonviolent mass resistance, and 8,500 people participate **1955** The ANC creates the Congress of the People, representing all races, and writes the Freedom Charter to end discrimination against blacks **1956** Mandela is arrested and tried in the "Treason Trial" **1956** Sudan wins independence from Britain, and Tunisia and Morocco gain independence from France **1959** Civil war breaks out in Rwanda between the two major tribes, Hutus and Tutsis

When	What
1960s	**1960** Police fire on protestors in Sharpeville, killing 69
	1960 European colonial powers grant independence to the African countries Chad, Gabon, Mauritania, Niger, Nigeria, Senegal, Togo, the French Congo, and the Ivory Coast
	1962 Independence for Algeria and Uganda
	1963 Kenya gains its independence from Britain
	1963 In America, Martin Luther King, Jr., gives his famous "I have a dream" speech
	1964 Mandela is convicted of sabotage and treason and sentenced to life in prison
	1968 Martin Luther King, Jr., is assassinated
1970s	**1972** Ethnic violence continues in Rwanda
	1975 Mozambique gains its independence from Portugal
	1978 Stephen Biko, the young leader of the Black Consciousness Movement in South Africa, dies in police custody
1980s	**1980** Oliver Tambo, in exile, launches an international campaign for Mandela's release from prison
	1983 Black residents near Johannesburg hold protests and many are killed by police
	1985 In America, rallies are held to support Nelson Mandela
	1989 F.W. de Klerk becomes president of South Africa and abolishes some apartheid policies
1990s	**1990** President F.W. de Klerk lifts the ban on the ANC and releases Mandela from prison
	1990 Namibia, formerly part of South Africa, is granted independence
	1993 Mandela and F.W. de Klerk are awarded the Nobel Peace Prize
	1993 Another outburst of ethnic violence in Rwanda/Burundi
	1994 Mandela is elected president of South Africa
	1999 Mandela steps down and Thabo Mbeki becomes president

On the Web

"MANDELA: AN AUDIO HISTORY" NPR

www.npr.org/templates/story/story.php?storyId=1851882

Listen to an amazing audio series about the life and work of Nelson Mandela. The series covers stories of Mandela's underground work against apartheid, his imprisonment, and South Africa's eventual democracy.

"MY HERO," WRITTEN BY MUHAMMAD ALI AT MYHERO.COM

http://myhero.com/myhero/hero.asp?hero=Ali_Mandela_bk06

At this site, you can read why world-famous boxer Muhammad Ali chose Nelson Mandela as his hero. You can also learn about heroes from all walks of life and even create a web page about your personal hero.

"ONLY THE TRUTH CAN PUT THE PAST TO REST" TIME FOR KIDS

www.timeforkids.com/TFK/teachers/wr/article/0,27972,89921,00.html

Read more about apartheid and how Mandela and the Truth and Reconciliation Commission worked to right the wrongs of South Africa.

"AROUND THE WORLD: SOUTH AFRICA" TIME FOR KIDS

www.timeforkids.com/TFK/teachers/aw/wr/article/0,28138,590849,00.html

Everything you want to know about the country of South Africa can be found at this interactive site. There's a sightseeing guide where you can check out some of South Africa's coolest places, a history timeline, a Question and Answer session with Nelson Mandela, and more.

At the Library

APARTHEID IN SOUTH AFRICA

by Michael J. Martin (Lucent Books, 2006)

This photo-illustrated book covers all aspects of apartheid, the segregationist policy in South Africa. Learn more about the African National Congress, Stephen Biko, Nelson Mandela, the Soweto uprising, Desmond Tutu, P.W. Botha, and more in this in-depth look at apartheid.

NELSON MANDELA'S FAVORITE AFRICAN FOLKTALES

edited by Nelson Mandela (W. W. Norton, 2007)

This wonderfully illustrated book contains thirty-two short African tales from all areas of the continent. The folktales, such as "The Snake with Seven Heads," "The Cloud Princess," and "The Ring of the King," were all chosen by Mandela himself.

HEROES AND VILLAINS: NELSON MANDELA

by Andy Koopmans (Lucent Books, 2004)

Mandela's life from birth to retirement is described in this interesting and well-written book. The book also features stories told in Mandela's own words

COUNTRIES OF THE WORLD: SOUTH AFRICA

by Mary-Ann Stotko (Gareth Stevens Publishing, 2002)

This book, loaded with photographs, takes an in-depth look at South Africa. It covers topics such as geography, history, people, conservation, arts, and food.

Y. kids

ISBN: 978-981-054944-2
May 2007

ISBN: 978-981-054945-9
June 2007

ISBN: 978-981-054942-8
May 2007

ISBN: 978-981-054943-5
June 2007

ISBN: 978-981-054946-6
July 2007

ISBN: 978-981-057555-7
May 2008

ISBN: 978-98105-4941-1
July 2007

ISBN: 978-981-057554-0
April 2008

ISBN: 978-981-057552-6
May 2008

ISBN: 978-981-057551-9
May 2008

ISBN: 978-981-057553-3
April 2008

ISBN: 978-981-057556-4
April 2008

EDUCATIONAL MANGA

ISBN: 981-05-2240-1

ISBN: 981-05-2241-X

ISBN: 981-05-2766-7

ISBN: 981-05-2765-9

ISBN: 981-05-2243-6

ISBN: 981-05-2238-X

ISBN: 981-05-2239-8

ISBN: 981-05-2768-3

ISBN: 981-005-2242-8

ISBN: 981-05-2767-5